Spooklights

The Amazing Cloverdale, Alabama
Spooklight Mystery

BY WYATT COX

~A GHOST RESEARCH SOCIETY PRESS PUBLICATION~

Original Cover Artwork Designed by
Jim Graczyk

This Book is Published by
Ghost Research Society Press
P.O. Box 205
Oak Lawn, Illinois, 60454
(708)-425-5163
http://www.ghostresearch.org

First Printing – 2007
ISBN: 0-9766072-8-X

Printed in the United States of America

Notice:

I have attempted to provide accurate and reliable information in this book. Due to the nature of this book, I assume no liability for any inaccuracies contained therein. The opinions expressed in this book are mine and I do not represent any of the people or organizations mentioned.

I encourage others to personally observe these amazing Spooklights and I also encourage those who venture to the sighting areas to obtain permission from the land owners before using their fields for a staging or camping area.

Acknowledgements

This book could not have been written without the valuable assistance and support from many talented people. It is virtually impossible for me to thank everyone who has contributed in some form to enable me to write this book.

Greg Keeton whom I have known since high school has been a true friend and without his encouragement and insatiable curiosity of the paranormal, I could not have even considered writing this book. When I refer to "we" in the book, I am referring to Greg.

His determination to explore and attempt to understand the Cloverdale Spooklights never diminished over the years. Many times we reached the same conclusions about the knowledge we learned; sometimes we did not. But we were always a team.

I am deeply indebted to the property owner (who wishes to remain anonymous) who has over the years has generously given Greg and me permission to use his land to view these Spooklights.

Many others have significantly influenced me over the years which greatly aided me in my long quest to understand the Cloverdale Spooklight phenomena. I was privileged to have met Dr. Thomas Bearden who is a well known scientist, prolific writer and engineer. He has offered many insights and ideas about the nature of Spooklights which I greatly appreciate and it is my opinion that his book *The Excalibur Briefing* should not only be considered a "classic" but is by far one of the best books I have read about the paranormal being explained from a scientist's perspective.

While I do not personally know William Corliss, it is his book, *Handbook of Unusual Natural Phenomena* which should be a "standard" for anyone who is interested in mysterious luminous phenomena. For me, this is the book which all other of this genre should be judged by.

Preface

Try to imagine yourself with some friends on a hill at the edge of a large field sitting in their lawn chairs beside a small but bright campfire. Darkness has already arrived and the sky is clear and there is a slight breeze out of the south. Hopefully the moon is hanging in the sky to chase away some of the darkness. The warm daytime temperature has now dropped by at least 10-15 degrees. You get up from your lawn chair and begin to pace.

You clutch the pair of binoculars around your neck and peer into the night sky. You briefly examine the moon and observe a plane in the distance. You are constantly moving your head, scanning the tree tops in the distance. Every now and then you hear a hound dog barking somewhere in the distance.

And then suddenly and without any advance notice, one of your friends who is doing the exact same thing you are doing, yells out with a sharp loud and excited voice, "there's a light! Over there!" At that instant everyone there with you in that large dark field, quickly and with an elevated level of adrenalin scans the sky and spots something that is so awesome that your mind instantly blocks out everything except one thing; and that is keeping your eyes firmly glued to that eight-foot diameter yellowish-orange pulsating sphere of bright light moving slowly above the tree tops in the distance about 1/3 of a mile away. Or perhaps it is floating above an adjacent field. Maybe it is low to the ground but is gaining altitude. Nevertheless, your eyes are fixed on the mysterious globe of bright yellowish-orange pulsating light.

Everyone is yelling something. The first question is "do you see it!?" And the second question is "are you using your camera!?" Hopefully someone notices what time the glowing orb was first noticed. The mysterious ball of light has a mesmerizing effect on the viewer and it takes a conscious effort to think about quickly running over to the tripod mounted camera and begin taking pictures.

The Spooklight is moving slowly. Sometimes it stops for no apparent reason and just "sits there" for several seconds before restarting its journey. The noticeable breeze from the south has no effect on its behavior. The Spooklight is very far away and it is strangely silent. The mysterious orb continues its journey and you become aware that it is pulsating with more intensity. The reason is unknown. Then it returns to its normal brightness and it still is moving slowly; its destination is a secret which it will never reveal. After about three to five minutes, the Spooklight has simply gone out of sight. Or maybe just as it suddenly appeared it suddenly disappeared. And then the sighting is over!

And while everyone is talking the Spooklight, they start again, scanning the skies.

And who knows, another Spooklight may soon appear! Or is it the same one returning for another performance?

Acknowledgments -1-

Preface -3-

CONTENTS

Note: While Spooklights have been called many things, such as Ghostlights, Aerial Luminous Phenomena, Lantern Lights, Earth Lights, etc, I have chosen to use the term Spooklight and to use the abbreviations of SL or SLs. Hopefully this designation will reduce possible confusion and keep things simple.

Acronyms:

I wish to include a few acronyms with the hope it will make the book more readable.

ASLSA

Active Spooklight Sighting Area

CSL

Cloverdale Spooklight

SL

Spooklight

Type 1 CSL

Type 1 is the typical yellowish-orange glowing orb that is about eight feet in diameter and can suddenly appear and disappear. It usually moves slow and has been known to stop and hover for several seconds. The SL is very bright and completely silent. About 90 percent are Type 1.

Type 2 CSL

This type of SL is about 4-6 feet in diameter and produces a dim white light. They usually move slightly faster than a Type 2 and are also silent. Less than three percent of all reported SLs are Type 2.

Type 3 CSL

This type is about the same diameter as the Type 2 SL and produces a dim blue light.
They also move faster than the Type 1 SLs. Greg and I have seen a total of four blue SLs.

OPC

Acronym for Old Prison Camp which is located about five miles east of highway 17 off CR 224 and where the Prison Camp Road ends. From I understand, the OPC was a minimum security prison that was operated until the mid 1960s. After its closure, there was no serious attempt to keep the facility operational. The buildings overtime deteriorated and many if not all have collapsed.

OPCA

Acronym for Old Prison Camp area. For Greg and me, it was any where within about ¾ miles or less from the boundaries of the Prison Camp

SLSA1

At the Tenn. State line on highway 17. Several good SLs have been seen at this area since the late 1970s and early 80s. They were all seen over looking a field which was about ¼ mile from the State Line, looking to the south. They traveled either west to east or east to west. Even though I have not personally been to this site in a quite a while, I assume it is still active since the other known areas are.

SLSA2

This location is about two miles south of the Old Prison Camp and can be accessed by turning east off of Highway 17 onto CR 24 and driving about four miles.

SLSA3

The Old Prison Camp (including adjacent fields) can be found by turning east off of Highway 17 onto CR 24. After crossing the Tennessee

Southern Railroad tracks, turn left onto Prison Camp Road (CR 311) which dead ends at the entrance gate for the prison.

SLSA4

This location can be accessed by traveling north from Florence on Highway 157 and turning east onto CR 141. In this area there are several large fields where the SLs can be seen. This area is actually due west from the Old Prison Camp.

Prologue

The quiet and pleasant city of Cloverdale is located in Lauderdale County which is in the northwestern corner of Alabama. In many ways it is just another southeastern town; lots of friendly and hospitable folks are proud to call this town home. Lauderdale County is tucked away in the state's extreme northwest corner; for it borders both Tennessee and Mississippi.

Cloverdale is a small metropolis with a total population of about 20,000 residents and is located on Highway 157, a few miles north of Florence. The terrain is typical for that part of the State. There are many gently rolling fields and forest land with an average elevation of about 600-650 feet above sea level. Many acres are dedicated to cattle ranches and various crops. The summers are hot and humid. And winters are sometimes cool. Snow accumulation is very rare. The average precipitation is bout 50 inches of rain per year. There are many streams and creeks which feed into the Tennessee River which is just a few miles south.

While the town and area may be typical in many respects, there is one unique feature about this area that I find very note worthy. And that is sometimes at night, large yellowish-orange bright glowing spheres of light can be seen floating above the trees or fields. These mysterious orbs are usually called Spooklights and it is my goal to share with the reader some things I have learned about these wondrous balls of light.

These Spooklights have been reported to appear as early as dusk and have been observed as late as 12:00 p.m. As many as eight Spooklights have been reported in a single night in one sighting area. Of course, there are some nights when none are seen. Over the years, Greg and I have identified two "kinds" of Cloverdale Spooklights. More than ninety-percent of them will be about eight-feet in diameter and are bright yellowish-orange to orange color. They all pulsate, move slowly and are completely silent. Some Spooklights are in sight for a few seconds while others are in clear view for more than eight minutes. The other "kind' of SL is visually different. They are much smaller and are either of a dim bluish or white color.

We are not sure if there are very few of the blue and white Spooklights or if they are few observed because they are more difficult to spot in the darkness. They also seem to ambulate at a slighter faster speed than the orange colored orbs. It is also possible that they are a "normal "Spooklight with little visible light or possible with less total energy.

To drive to a good viewing area is not a difficult task. And if a map is used to locate these sighting areas, it is quickly seen that these Spooklights almost always travel in an almost invisible "path" or "track" as though there is no option but to follow it.

The earliest accounts of these SLs that we know of go back to late 1972 when several folks began reporting watching orange (some reported red) balls of light floating across the night sky a short distance west of Lexington. From February through October of 1973, several hundreds of unidentified bright nocturnal lights were reported in and near a large land fill a short distance from Lexington. This small town is located a short distant south of the Tennessee State line and is due east of Cloverdale. They were seen at night and they were reported as not having blinking lights and were completely silent. Some would hover for a while and some would move fast across the sky. Others would be at tree top level and some would be much higher.

While I'm sure that some honest folks misidentified conventional aircraft flying, Venus, etc. I can't but wonder if a high percentage of these UFOs were not really SLs. After taking into account the obvious misidentifications of conventional aircraft, the descriptions of a lot of these UFO reports would be consistent of how a large SL would be described.

My current understanding is that in this "window" area large numbers of SLs are produced on a reoccurring basis; some are for the most part visible, and some are normally not visible. I make no claim that Spooklights are responsible for the entire UFO Phenomenon. For me, what ever natural energies are involved in the creation of these SLs, they are not directly associated with the UFO phenomenon – especially regarding the extraterrestrial spacecraft views.   But they are wondrous to watch!

A time exposure photo taken of a Spooklight near GLSA2 in the summer of 1979. This Spooklight was moving to the west at a slow speed and reached it maximum altitude as shown in this photo. It was in sight for about five minutes.

Introduction

I have reached the conclusion that all people love a good mystery. Mystery novels are sold by the millions each year. Many successful and classic movies and T.V shows are "mysteries." And who doesn't like to watch an old black and white Sherlock Holmes movie starring Basil Rathbone? The type of mystery that captivates one person may not be the type that captivates some one else. Perhaps we are attracted to a mystery because it deals with things and people that are unknown to us and it causes us to actively engage our imaginations. And we receive no enduring satisfaction until the mystery has been solved.

My "mystery" is very unusual and is not easy for me to explain. I make no dogmatic claims that I have solved this mystery. In fact, I really can't explain the mystery very well at all. I can only tell you about it with the hope that one day it will be satisfactorily solved and understood by those who are much smarter than me.

My "mystery" began in 1977 when my good friend (Greg Keeton) and I was informed by a mutual friend that his mother had seen several strange and large and bright yellowish-orange orbs near her house floating above some distant trees on several occasions. "Mom" quickly realized these strange lights were not airplanes since these balls of light were silent, had no blinking lights and would occasionally stop and hover. With each sighting, her curiosity intensified.

She actually first noticed these glowing spheres while inside her house looking out her kitchen window while washing the dinner dishes (I'm glad she did not have a dishwashing machine)! She had noticed these strange lights for several weeks and began mentioning her sightings to friends and family. Fortunately, her teenage son knew that Greg and I were interested in UFOs.

From that time until now, Greg and I remain immensely fascinated and mesmerized by this phenomenon. It is unlike anything else we have seen and we are not aware of any other Spooklight sighting area that compares to the ones in Cloverdale, Alabama.

My first exposure to the UFO phenomenon began in 1973 when north Alabama experienced a major UFO flap which lasted from February through November of that year. Actually many eastern states underwent a major UFO flap that year. It seemed that the local newspapers printed articles about UFO sightings nearly every day! UFOs were the talk of the town and almost everybody seemed compelled to form a strong opinion about them. And human nature being as it is, most folks felt like that had to choose sides. Oh, there were a few folks who claimed they were indifferent about the issue, but for the most part, people either said they believed in UFOs or they did not.

And during this time period, UFOs were almost exclusively associated with the alleged existence of physical space craft and aliens from outer space. And because of the prevailing conclusions about the nature of the UFO phenomenon, many good sightings went unreported for fear of the witnesses would be ridiculed. One of the most famous (or infamous!) UFO/alien sightings (without the UFO!) was reported in north Alabama on the night of October 17, 1973 when the sheriff of the small town of Falkville reported (and photographed) observing a "robot" (most of us Alabamians refer to the "robot" as the Tin Foil Man) running in a field near an area where a large glowing UFO had reportedly been seen earlier that night.

Whether Sheriff Grenhaw actually saw an alien or was a victim of a clever hoax has been debated for more than three decades. And I have no wish to wade into this debate. But the fact is, when the topic of UFOs came up for discussion, there was no way to separate the UFO from the alien astronauts who were for unknown reasons visiting us from outer space.

As a fourteen-year-old in 1973 I was fortunate to had relatives living in an area (Lexington area) where many UFOs sightings were reported, and was able to visit them often. I actually saw my first unidentified orange light back in the spring of that year. It was nothing spectacular – just a spherical shaped ball of light in the distance. To this day, I tend to believe it was a Spooklight.

It was at this time my interest was kindled. And it was also about at this time I met Greg Keeton, a life long friend who also has the same fascination (or can I say addiction!) with the Cloverdale Spooklight.

Since I became aware of their existence in the late 1970s, the Cloverdale Spooklights have held a strong fascination for me. In fact, there was a time when I would more likely say the word compulsion instead of fascination. Why get hooked on phonetics when you can get hooked on Spooklights. Once a person views an eight-foot diameter yellowish-orange Spooklight gently, and slowly floating above the trees – the feelings are difficult to describe. But after watching a Spooklight, the question I would ask myself is, when can I see another one!?

From 1977 to 1982, Greg and I spent more than one hundred and fifty nights out in various fields looking for Spooklights. During this period of time, we narrowed down the better sighting areas to four locations. All four locations are within about six miles of each other and fortunately two of the sighting areas are easily accessible to the public. These locations actually form a triangle (well almost) extending from Tennessee, about a mile west of Highway 17, southward to Cloverdale and eastward to St. Florian. While several Spooklights have been seen outside of this triangle, the majority of the SLs we have observed were seen inside it boundaries. I actually consider the Spooklights to be observed in a "window" which is part of what I sometimes call a Spooklight Corridor.

Thankfully, Greg and I have permission from the land owners to access and use the properties of two of these locations (this doesn't mean we trespassed at the other locations!). There are several other areas where these Spooklights can be seen from, but for practical reasons, we now use these two locations. Since the Spooklights may travel up to a mile or more before disappearing or floating away from our line of sight, several other viewing areas also exist.

After 1981, with my job and school, Greg and I had no choice but to curtail our many nightly visits to watch the Spooklights. In 1984, I began moving a lot with my job and only on the occasional visit to Florence would I have the opportunity to watch a Spooklight. Greg continued to make a few trips out to the viewing areas and usually would be rewarded with several good sightings.

As the years passed, so did our opportunities to continue our "fascination." Eventually Greg and I decided to renew (even though on a limited scope) our efforts to observe and document more Spooklights and hopefully learn what produces these amazing glowing orbs.

While I currently live in South Carolina, I am able to make one to two trips a year to Florence where my parents live. Greg and I still attempt to go to the sighting areas and when we do we usually have some good sightings.

Even now we and others who know where to go can still see these large orange pulsating globes of orange light. Whatever is causing this phenomenon has been doing so for more than 30 years and there is no indication of any change in its trends, appearance, behavior, etc.

Time exposure photo of eight-foot diameter Spooklight moving across the sky near GLSA2. There is an airplane in the distance below the SL. Photographed by Wyatt Cox.

History

UFOs have been reported in northern Alabama for a long time. Most are seen at night and are reported as unidentified nocturnal lights. It is not yet clear to me which UFOs are Spooklights and which are not. As with a high percentage of UFO sightings; they occur at night. I suspect that most nocturnal UFOs which are reported as being solid colored yellowish-orange lights are in fact SLs. I do know that beginning in the early 1970s a major UFO flap occurred in the northwestern region of Alabama. The flap's epicenter appeared to be a short distance from Lexington.

The evidence also supports the view that these Spooklights have been in Lauderdale County for many years. There a number of reasons I believe the Spooklights are a long term reoccurring phenomena. One reason is that they have been seen since at least the early 1970s by numerous independent witnesses. And since they have been around for more than three decades, it seems to me that what ever energies are responsible for their formation would have been in existence for a much longer period of time.

According to the February 08, 1973 edition of the *East Lauderdale News,*

"Unidentified Flying Objects have been seen recently in the East Lauderdale Area." The article indicates that several witnesses had observed numerous UFOs during the past several nights. Whether these

UFOs are actually Spooklights is debatable. However, when one examines the "path" the SLs generally follow, it seems very reasonable that at least some of these UFOs were SLs.

What is interesting is the writer of this article has a caption for a photo of the area where the orbs were being seen which says *"UFO AIRPORT? Lexington Land Fill has been the scene of many UFO "sightings" lately."* And guess what the headline for the article is: *"Garbage Dump-UFO!"* According to the writer of this article "hundreds" of people have reported observing nocturnal sightings of UFOs near Lexington.

According to staff writer Lucille Prince's article (entitled *UFO Capers Continue, Saucer Lands In Field*) in the February 18, 1973 edition of the **Florence Times**, Raleigh Nix and four other witnesses spotted a very large ball of light near their house at 11:30 p.m. According to the article, Nix claims the large orb was about 900 feet from his house when it landed in a field and the mysterious light was slightly larger than a car. He also claimed that the glowing orb was "…so bright it almost hurt your eyes to look at it." After a few moments, the glowing sphere suddenly vanished. Nix also claimed this was not his first sighting of this strange glowing orb.

Author's Note:

Greg and I interviewed Raleigh Nix in 1978 about this sighting and were able to visit the field where the strange glowing orb was seen. All that Raleigh told us about the Spooklight sighting was consistent with Prince's article. Nix claimed he and four other adults observed a large bright ball of light hovering in a field for a few moments and then it began to slowly "float" across the field. The orb remained about two to three feet above the ground and then it suddenly disappeared.

I remain convinced that they observed a very bright Spooklight just like the others seen between Lexington and Cloverdale.

The Florence Times reported in their March 19, 1973 edition that a policeman reported spotting a large UFO near Haleyville. The title of the article is *"Haleyville Resident Says UFO Reported: "Was Big As A Bus.""* The police officer claimed that it was "…the most amazing thing I have ever seen."

While I cannot ascertain that officer actually sighted a SL, it is definitely a possibility based on the description of the object.

According to the April 09, 1973 edition of *Florence Times* newspaper, Hal Cooper and [1]Bill Rogers observed a UFO near the Lexington landfill. According to the [2]article,

"The object appeared oval in shape, had no blinking lights (as others had reported), and varied slightly in color from yellowish orange to yellowish white." Both witnesses observed the silent object moving "slowly across the sky" and it suddenly disappeared when it crossed a nearby road.

---

[1] At the time, Bill Rogers was a college student and a member of the *Aerial Phenomena Research Organization.*

[2] Name of article is *"Couple Of Frat Brothers See UFO."*

According to staff writer Tony Kessler's article (entitled Officers Sight 'Ball of Light' Near Florence") of the *Florence Times* in the October 12, 1976 edition, two police officers watched a "ball of light" fall "…from 50 degrees above the horizon until it was completely out of sight."

The "ball of light" was first sighted at 6:30 p.m. by the two officers while near Coffey High School. One of the officers radioed four others who also watched the mysterious glowing phenomenon slowing decrease its altitude until it was out of sight. The glowing orb was in sight for about twenty minutes.

Greg and I saw our first SL on March 24, 1977, a short distance from the small and tranquil community of St. Florian. We had already been told about these mysterious lights by a friend's mother, so Greg and I along with our friend and his mother convened at the sighting area that night just as darkness approached. We were excited and somewhat apprehensive. Little did we know that our "addiction" was about to begin!

At 9:21 p.m. (we know the time because Greg kept a detailed journal of our sightings) a very bright amber colored Spooklight suddenly appeared to the west, just hovering in the distance above some trees. There was no blinking or flashing lights – just the large bright yellowish-orange light hanging in the sky! It was not something with a bright light. It was not a physical object with a bright light. The glowing sphere was a bright light! Its apparent size was much larger than Venus would be in the night sky and it definitely was not Venus. It was an actual ball of light. At the time, we had no idea that the SL actually pulsated with varying intensity. To our surprise the SL suddenly began to move in a southeast direction, and then it stopped and hovered again, even though there was a slight breeze. After hovering for maybe a full minute, it resumed its course but we noticed that the orb was beginning to lose altitude. Within two minutes, it went out of sight behind some trees and was not seen again.

We were totally ecstatic! We had just witnessed a UFO! Yet we already suspected it was not a typical UFO because it did not appear to be an "object" in the normal sense of the word. But nonetheless, and unknown to us at that time, our journey had just begun!

Four days later Greg, a mutual friend and I attempted to the see a SL again. This time we were in a slightly different location, hoping to get a better and closer view. We arrived shortly after dark. The sky was completely void of clouds and a bright crescent Moon was high above the horizon. And what a night that was! We did not see just one SL but saw a total of five! This night ties for third as far as viewing the most SLs in a single night.

The first one appeared at 9:22 p.m. and was in sight for about six minutes. When we first saw the bright orange orb, it was hovering about 200 feet from the ground in the distance. After a short time, it began to move away in a southwest to southeast trajectory and it became much brighter. It finally moved outside our field of vision.

The second SL appeared at 9:40 p.m. and was in sight for five minutes. It was bright orange moved in a straight line in a north to south direction. This one did not hover or change its speed. The nocturnal orb traveled a straight line to the east and was perhaps ¾ miles away when we first saw it. We guessed that it was about 300 feet from the ground.

The third SL was appeared just immediately after the second one flew out of sight (we noticed this odd "coincidence" several times). This one acted strangely in that it changed speed and brightness and flew in a zigzag pattern part of the time. When it began to fly in a straight line, we noticed something we have not seen on any other SLs: there was some kind of glowing "discharge" which reminded us of a short smoke trail.

The fourth SL appeared immediately after the third one went out of sight. This was at 9:50 p.m. This one was also a very bright orange and was more typical in behavior. It did change brightness and moved slowly to the west. This orb was in sight for about five minutes.

Then at 10:00 p.m. the fifth one appeared and it seemed larger (could have been brighter) than the others. Most likely it was not larger, just a little closer. However, we could not verify our hunch. This one was not yellowish-orange but rather reddish-orange. It seemed to be traveling parallel to a nearby road, so we quickly jumped into my car and attempted to follow it, but was not successful. It flew out of site within a minute or so.

Greg and I spent many hours in 1977 watching SLs and attempting to find the best viewing areas. We also interviewed several adults who had also seen them. We began to figure out where and when to go to watch these amazing orange orbs.

A summary of our sightings in 1977 is:

Date	Number of Spooklights seen
March 24	One
March 28	Five
April 08	Two
May 24	One
June 03	Three
August 05	One
August 26	One
Sept. 23	One
Oct. 14	One
Nov. 04	One

Dec. 16	One
Dec. 19	One

Total number of Spooklights Greg and I observed together in 1977 is nineteen. Of course, there were some nights Greg and I did not see any SLs. Since March 24, 1979 until the present, Greg and I have seen more than 180 Spooklights. In many instances, we had friends with us who witnessed several of these SLs.

One other remarkable sighting occurred on April 16, 1980 near a large field, a short distance from the "old prison camp." Actually we saw three SLs that night but one did something that we have not ever seen prior to this sighting or any sighting since then.

It was the last of the three SLs to appear. It suddenly materialized at 8:51 p.m. and was in sight for about four minutes. There was nothing unusual about this SL – until it "broke off" into two SLs of almost equal size and brightness. All of a sudden, the one SL became two SLs! The slightly smaller orb (about six feet in diameter) floated a mere three-five feet directly under the slightly larger one for about 200-300 feet. And then the two orbs quickly merged and became one again and continued on its (them!) merry way! There was no sound, unusual pulsations (that we could see) or anything else unusual. The question I ask is did the one become two for a short time or were there two SLs traveling together all along, but became separate for a short time? And if so, why? Now you see why Greg and I are addicted to Spooklights!

The most SLs we have seen in a single night were eight on November 7, 1980. All were bright orange and were typical SLs. While all were about eight feet in diameter, some flew at lower altitudes than others and some flew slower than others. Seven SLs were seen by Greg and me on January 24, 1980 and five on March 6, 1980. Why were so many SLs seen in 1980? It is difficult for me to say. One possible reason is that Greg and I spent more time in the field that year than in 1977 or 1978.

Time exposure photo of a bright Spooklight seen at SLSA2. It was large and moved slowly towards the west. Photograph by Wyatt Cox

Characteristics of the Cloverdale Spooklights

There are several characteristics of the Cloverdale Spooklights we have observed since 1977 and they include:

1. All of the yellowish-orange (or amber) Spooklights are about eight-feet in diameter. Very few appear larger or smaller. We have been close enough to the CSLs to know for certain they are usually about eight feet in diameter. Many other independent witnesses have also made this claim.

2. All (only a few have been seen) of the dull bluish colored Spooklights appear to be about 2-3 feet in diameter. None appear larger and none appear smaller. It is possible they are much larger, but the visible portion (presumably the center) is about this size. Only a few have been seen and in the darkness they are sometimes difficult to spot. They also seem to move slightly faster than the orange Spooklights.

3. All the yellowish-orange Spooklights are silent. No sound of any kind has ever been associated with this phenomenon.

4. All the orange Spooklights pulsate. It may not be apparent to the naked eye, but when using visual aids, it is more evident. Some may appear to flicker but they are actually pulsating.

5. All the SLs are subject to suddenly appearing and disappearing. Many that disappear do so for just a few seconds and suddenly become visible again. Rarely does a SL give advance indication that it is going to vanish from view. Occasionally a Spooklight will begin to "flicker" for a few seconds but if it does, the orb most will most likely will "go out" at least for a few moments if not permanently.

6. The longevity of a Spooklight is not predictable. Some are visible for only a few seconds and some are in sight for up to eight minutes.

7. They travel at a relatively slow rate of speed. Greg and I estimate the average speed is about 20- 30 MPH. Of course, it is not uncommon for a SL to stop and hover for a short time.

8. Their altitude is not predictable. A few have been seen just a few feet above the ground and some have been quite high – perhaps 2,000 feet. Several witnesses (including Greg and I) have reported seeing Spooklight a mere two feet above the ground. On one

occasion (The Spooklight Crashed story) a CSL was actually seen to "crash" in a heavily wooded area.

9. How many will be seen on a given night is not predictable (but there are established trends). Usually about two will be seen on a given night but this is a generalization. On some nights Greg and I did not see any Spooklight and on some nights we have seen as many as eight.

A pattern I mentioned is that more are seen from October through April. Fewer are seen June through August, even though some of the better sightings have occurred during the summer. We cannot prove that summer temperatures directly affect the formation of Spooklight. Perhaps the higher temperature somehow acts as a squelching agent. Yet there must be a reason for the decrease in activity. If this phenomenon is produced by subterranean electrical fields, then it is possible that a lower ground water table during the summer might be a contributing factor.

10. There does not appear to be any other "paranormal" activity in or near our sighting areas. We are not aware of any "real" UFOs (the ET types) seen in the Spooklight's "path." There are the "usual" paranormal phenomena in northern Alabama just like there are in any other areas. One active paranormal organization in north Alabama is the Alabama Foundation for Paranormal Research and their web site is alabamaparanormal.org. And while Greg and I

have investigated a house reported to be haunted and investigated a good Bigfoot sighting reported by three witnesses in Athens (a mid sized town about forty miles east of Cloverdale), I generally hold to this view, yet, perhaps the jury is still out on this issue.

11. Some if not all of the yellowish-orange Spooklights may have a smaller and dimmer light connected to the primary light. Greg and I discovered this unknown characteristic recently when we shot a video of a Spook light in February, 2006.

Up until this time, we had no idea there was a smaller much dimmer light attached to the main body. Yet we have on about three occasions observed a "piece" of the Spooklight break off and fall a short distance and then disappear. Now we suspect that it was the secondary light which became separated and was pulled away by gravity.

They are not affected by the wind. Greg and I have viewed some Spooklights during very windy conditions. Never have we noticed any being affected by a brisk breeze. We have seen a few that shimmered in a strong breeze but their speed and course remained unaltered. Even one that stops and hovers will hold its stationary position regardless of wind speed.

12. They all (with very few exceptions) travel on a specific a "path" which means once a Spooklight is sighted its "path" can be quickly

determined. And if other Spooklights are seen in that same location most likely they all will travel the same identical route. Their deviation if any will be less than a mile. This is one of the more remarkable aspects of the Spooklights.

Additional Observations and Comments

1) We have found no evidence of Spooklights interfering with man made electrical/electronics systems. Either their energy is **A**) not intense enough, **B**) not near enough, or **C**) does not possess the attributes that would produce interference. The temperature of these Spooklights does not appear (no scientific tests have been performed) to be significantly different than the ambient temperature. On one occasion, Greg and I (and others) watched a Spooklight rapidly descend from about 500 feet and "crashed" into some nearby woods. Upon arriving at the "crash" site, we found no evidence of any charred or heat damaged vegetation. The Spooklight simply disappeared when it impacted the ground. It can also be argued that the reason for the "crash" is that the SL did not maintain sufficient thermal energy and lost its ability to remain intact.

2) We are not aware of any Spooklights "going through" buildings, communication towers, or other solid objects.

3) Another odd aspect to these Spooklights is that it "appears" that some of them become dimmer or temporarily disappear if an airplane is in the nearby vicinity. Once the airplane has flown past the area of the Spooklight, it either becomes brighter or reappears. We are still scratching our heads on this. My summary of some of the more puzzling aspects of the Cloverdale SL phenomenon are: If the CSLs are randomly formed by the complex interactions or mediation of two or more of the various natural energies (electromagnetic fields, cosmic radiation, telluric currents, etc.) in the area, and are not directly affected by manmade electrical devices or electrical fields produced by humans, then why is it that they have not been known to have formed or seen:

1) In habitable structures (e.g. houses, churches, schools, etc.)?

2) Near a habitable structure (within 200 feet)?

3) Near a person (within 200 feet)?

4) On a road?

5) Beside an automobile?

6) Beside a farm animal?

7) At communications towers?

8) At high voltage power lines?

While I hold to the above statement, I did interview a man who claimed that when he was a teenager in 1973, he observed a UFO a short distance west of Lexington hovering about forty feet above a high voltage transmission line and its supporting steel tower. I personally know this man well enough to consider him a credible witness. I include this commentary because evidence should not be discarded merely because it does not fit neatly into one's personal views.

9) At low voltage power lines for residential areas?

10) Above the various electrical generating stations in the region (Wilson and Wheeler Dams – both operated by the Tennessee Valley Authority)? Of course one could argue that they may indeed exist in some of these locations, but are not producing visible radiation. It appears this argument is possibly valid – but currently is supported only by conjecture and indirect evidence. All of the viewing areas that I mention in this book are privately owned except for the prison camp property which is owned by the city of Florence. While I encourage others to view these wondrous

glowing orbs, I do not encourage anyone to trespass on private property. The good news is that there are several public roads where the SLS can be seen. And if serious researchers are interested, I may be able to obtain permission from the land owners for those to access the viewing areas.   Greg and I would ask ourselves if there were multiple SLs or if they were but a few and they were traveling several miles before disappearing. We wondered if the SL that was seen at SLSA1 was also being seen a few minutes later at SLSA3 since they would usually travel in a south to south east direction.

On a few occasions I would be at SLSA1 and he would be at SLSA2 to hopefully determine the distance a SL would travel. We both concluded that the information gathered did not support the position that there were only a few SLs being produced even though we suspected a few travel (visibly) up to five miles or so.

We have also noticed that by drawing a straight line due east from the Cloverdale sighting area, the line will cross the SLSA3, SLSA4 and the small town of Lexington which underwent a major UFO flap in 1973. And as a "coincidence," more than 90% of the Lexington UFOs reported fall into the nocturnal lights category which means several of these could have been SLs.   I also realize there are other possible explanations for the hundreds of UFO sightings reported in the Lexington area in 1973.

There were a few times when we suspected that some nearby dogs would begin barking just prior to us spotting a SL. Sometimes there seemed to be at least a casual connection. But over the years, we can not really establish a direct link to the spontaneous barking of dogs and a SL sighting. But can us with total confidence rule out the possibility that the invisible SL may produce very high or very low frequency sounds and the visible ones do not? At this time, I have no direct evidence to support this view. My "gut" am telling me dogs don't need a reason to bark. Dogs are going to bark just because they are dogs!

Based on our experiences and interviews with other witnesses, we have concluded that SLs do not leave any physical evidence. The SL we saw "crash" into a wooded area is an example. We also interviewed witnesses who observed a SL either on the ground or hovering 1-2 feet from the ground and left no evidence of its presence, such as scorched grass, discolored soil, etc.

As to how much energy is present in a Spooklight is unknown. It would seem that to produce a very bright eight-foot diameter sphere of light, a fair amount of electrical energy would be present. It would seem to me that at least a few kilowatts would be necessary to produce and maintain a Spooklight. With the proper instrumentation, this question could be answered.

Investigating the Cloverdale Spooklights: 1) The Early Years and 2) Recent Times

This chapter includes many but not all of our sightings from 1977 through 1980 which I refer to as the early years. This compilation does not include the nights (there were several) we visited the viewing areas and did not observer SLs.

March 24, 1977

Greg and I arrived together in my car at a friend's house because his mother had been viewing large orange glowing spheres floating about 100 feet above some trees area near her house on an almost nightly basis for more than two weeks. We were asked to come and observe the strange orange balls of light because she knew Greg and I were interested in UFOs. She was also hoping that Greg and I could help explain to her what the strange orbs were.

The strange lights would normally appear out of the west above a large wooded area and travel east on the same "path" beginning at sunset. Several of the large orbs would be seen floating perhaps 200-400 feet above the ground.

We wanted to be at her house earlier than when we expected to see this strange orb so we actually "scouted out" the area first and then drove to her house about an hour before sunset and then attempted to find the best viewing area. Our friend "John" and his mother remained with us and she shared her accounts of the other Spooklights see had seen.

All of us gathered in her front yard and began watching and talking. The evening sky was overcast with high altitude clouds so no stars were visible. There was a slight wind out of the south and the moon would occasionally almost peek through an opening in the fragmented cloud cover. And there at the north end of a very large field, we watched and waited. At 9:21 p.m. we were amply rewarded with a very good sighting.

A bright SL suddenly (and I mean suddenly!) appeared just above a wooded area to our south. The SL was very bright yellowish-orange and was hovering. It did not appear in the distance and floated into view at the other end of the field. Instead, the SL was just there; hanging in the air above some trees! One moment we saw nothing over the trees to our south and the next instant, it was there! The glowing orb was very large; at least eight feet across may have been ½ to ¾ miles from us. After a few seconds of the orb hovering above the trees, it began to move slowly towards the southeast. The SL then increased it speed for a few seconds and then it suddenly stopped and hovered for about one minute. The yellowish-orange ball of light began to move again and this time it was gradually losing altitude and after a more few minutes, it went out of sight behind some trees. This glowing mystery orb was in sight for about nine minutes. This was my first time to actually watch one of these wondrous glowing orbs. And from this time forward, Greg and I were "hooked" on these mysterious balls of light.

March 28, 1977

Greg and I with two friends go back to where we observed our first Spooklight and walked further into the grassy field with the hope of being in a better viewing area. We actually decided on a spot about ½ miles from our original location. On this night, the sky was clear and a crescent moon was seen to our east. At 9:22 p.m. we all noticed a large yellowish-orange SL hovering about a half-mile away to our south. It was as though someone had simply turned of a light switch! One moment there was not a glowing ball of light and the next moment it was there.

We estimated that it was about 200-300 feet from the ground. It was past the field where we were standing and was above a large densely wooded area. After just a few seconds the SL began to move towards the southeast and as it traveled, its brightness constantly fluctuated as though it was pulsing. After about six minutes it had moved too far way and was out of sight.

At 9:40 p.m. we spotted another bright orange SL at a fairly high altitude and moved in a straight line towards the south. Its speed and brightness remained constant for five minutes and then it had moved too far away to view it.

Just as this one was no longer in sight, another one appeared and was moving towards the southeast at a slow speed. But this SL behaved quiet differently; while it was in sight for five minutes, it moved in a zigzag fashion for about half of the time we saw it. Another unique feature was that it produced what appeared to be a short orange colored smoke trail. We estimated that this SL was about ¾ of a mile from us when it first appeared.

This is the only time we have seen a SL produce a trail of any kind. Was the air directly behind it electrically charged? Was this discharge some how involved in propelling it through the air?

When this SL was becoming too far away to see, another one suddenly appeared out of the west and was moving slowly towards the east. This one was also about eight feet in diameter and was bright orange. We noticed it gaining speed as it moved away from us and it brightness also varied in intensity. It was in sight for about five minutes before leaving our field of vision.

At 10:00 p.m. a large reddish-orange SL appeared just past the field we were in. It was perhaps 300 feet from the ground and was moving very slow. We could see that if the SL continued its course, it would pass over a nearby road, and would float across another field parallel to the road. We quickly jumped into our car and attempted to follow the large glowing ball of light. But when we arrived at the spot where we should have seen the SL, it was not there. Either we had misjudged the SL's flight path or it change directions. Either way we were able to watch the SL in the distance continue its journey and after about a minute it had flown away.

April 08, 1977

On this night, Greg and I decided to actually go inside the Old Prison Camp and set up an observation station on a high spot in an open area near its north side. Two friends came with us who had already seen some Spooklights in the area.

At 9:25 p.m. we noticed a very bright yellowish-orange SL moving below some trees in the distance and it was moving slowly in a straight line. Based on the gently rolling terrain, we guessed it was less than 200 feet from the ground. The SL was about eight feet in diameter and about ½ a mile from us. The SL remained in view for about five minutes before it was out of sight.

May 24, 1977

Greg and I experimented with a different position this time and which was about a mile from an unused prison camp that is usually referred to as the "Old Prison Camp (OPC)." We arrived at the edge of a large empty field which was a short distance from the camp. The sky was partly cloudy and a half-moon was hanging in the sky. We were about ready to pack up and head home when at 10:45 p.m. we noticed that a large orange SL appeared over some trees about ¾ of mile from us. The bright light moved slowly in a straight line over some mature hardwoods and was going towards the southeast. It was in sight for two minutes.

June 03, 1977

On this night, Greg and I with three friends went to the field that borders the north side of the OPC and selected a slightly elevated spot to set up our gear. We arrived at 6:00 p.m. The sky was completely void of clouds and only the stars offered us any nighttime light. At 9:15 p.m. we spotted a bright orange SL above some tall trees to the west. It was large and moving slowly to the southeast and was about 300 feet from the ground. After about four minutes, it had moved out of visual range.

At 9:40 p.m. we spotted another large orange orb flying much higher and moving very slowly towards the southeast. It seemed just as large as the other SL and was in sight for nine minutes. We did not notice any change in brightness or erratic movements.

About one minute after this SL was out of sight a small blue ball of light appeared and was moving towards the southeast. It seemed to be on the same course as the previous SL, but because it was smaller, we could not really guess its altitude or speed. We do know that it moved at a low rate of speed because it was in sight for almost six minutes. These rare and blue orbs are obviously related to the large orange SLs, but we remain perplexed about these phenomena.

August 05, 1977

Greg and I with two friends are back at the large field on the north side of the OPC. The sky was clear except for some clouds to our southeast. Being summer, the air was still, hot and very humid. There was no moon to offer us any nighttime illumination. From 8:00 to 9:35 p.m. we waited. And then a large orange orb suddenly emerged from a wooded area about ½ miles away and was moving slow but was quickly gaining altitude. It moved upward for a few seconds and then it stopped and hovered for about one minute. As the SL hovered, its intensity suddenly and noticeable increased and then it immediately began moving straight up for about 100 feet and then made a 90 degree turn and flew horizontal. The SL began to move much faster and after a couple of minutes it was out of sight behind a distant wooded area.

August 26, 1977

Greg and I went to a different field which is about three miles west of the OPC. We wanted to find the best viewing areas and we knew we could accomplish this goal by trial and error. We arrived just before dark and began to watch. The sky was peppered with low thick clouds and a half-moon occasionally peeked through and offered us some light. At 9:35 p.m. we spotted a typical large orange SL moving slowly to the south. It was actually a very good sighting and the orb was about 200 feet from the ground as it moved in a straight line above the rolling terrain. These SL was in sight for about four minutes.

September 23, 1977

Greg and I went to a different location that is about two miles from the OPC. The sky was littered with some thin high altitude clouds. At 9:21 p.m. we noticed that a large orange SL had appeared over some trees about a ½ mile to our west and began to move toward the southeast. As it gradually gained elevation, it increased its speed and its brightness. The SL also began to fluctuate. It would be very bright one moment and very dim another. This continued for about two minutes. When its ascent had leveled out and it started moving horizontally, the SL's pulsations become odder; almost becoming totally invisible and quickly becoming extremely bright. It then suddenly "went out" and was not seen again.

September 30, 1977

Greg and I went back to the same location we were at the week earlier. While it was dark, Wilson High School which was some distance away was having a homecoming ballgame and their bright lights for the ball field were on and they limited our viewing range. At 9:56 p.m. we spotted a bright orange orb moving fairly fast above some distant trees. It had appeared to our south and seemed to be following highway 17. After watching the glowing sphere for two minutes, it suddenly vanished.

October 14, 1977

Greg and I returned to the field mentioned above for hopefully another excellent sighting. We arrived at 7:30 p.m. and began to watch. The sky was littered with scattered clouds and there was a slight cool wind. At 9:33 p.m. a large and very bright orange SL suddenly appeared about ½ mile from us above some trees and moved very slowly to the southeast. It remained about 200 feet from the ground as it crossed several fields and wooded areas. These SL was in sight for about five minutes before moving out of sight.

November 04, 1977

Greg and I decided to go to the back side of a large grassy field that is near some rail road tracks (The Tennessee-Southern railroad tracks) that run a short distance to the north of the OPC. Two of our friends arrived a few minutes after we did. We had to park about 1/3 of a mile from our observation site. The sky was partly cloudy and there was a slight breeze out of the north. At 9:02 p.m. we spotted an extremely bright (the brightest one we have ever seen) orange SL moving very slowly towards the southeast. It was about 150 feet from the ground and began to decrease its elevation. This SL was somewhat odd because it did not appear to be a true sphere, but was somewhat elongated. As it came to tree top level, the bottom part of the SL became very dim yet the top half retained its original brightness. And a few seconds later, it simply "went out." This SL was in sight for about two minutes.

December 16, 1977

Greg and I with and three other friends arrived in a field behind the Old Prison Camp just as the sun was setting. The sky was filled with high thin clouds and there was a strong breeze out of the north. There was a one-quarter moon trying to peek through the clouds. We saw one SL that night and it appeared at 9:00 p.m. and was in sight for just twenty seconds. This one was farther away than normal and was flying just below he trees in the distance which obstructed our view of the orb. It was typical in both size and color.

December 19, 1977

Greg and I returned to the field near the Old Prison Camp with the hopes of a better night. Just as our previous trip, there was a brisk wind out of the north. As usual for this time of year, Greg and I made a camp fire for both light and especially for some welcomed heat.

We watched just one SL on this night as well. It appeared at 9:15 p.m. and was in sight for forty seconds. It was not as near as we had hoped and it was flying low enough for the trees in the distance to partially obstruct our view.

March 04, 1978

Greg and I along with four other friends were stationed in a field near the Old Prison Camp. The sky was clear and a slight but cold breeze reminded us that spring had not yet arrived. We arrived at bout 7:30 p.m. and built a small camp fire. At 8:42 p.m. we all noticed a bright reddish-orange orb moving towards the southwest. This one was similar to several others; it just suddenly appeared and was actually flying just above some nearby trees. Its speed varied and once it stopped and hovered for more than two minutes before resuming its course. This SL eventually moved out of sight rather than suddenly disappear as many have done. The SL was in sight for a total of six minutes. We were able to take several photos of this SL with a Pentax camera mounted on a tripod.

March 06, 1978

Greg and I drove to a field very close to the Old Prison Camp with three friends. The sky was peppered with high altitude clouds and there was a slight breeze out of the north. On this night we spotted two bright SLs.

The first one appeared at 8:44 p.m. and was in sight for two minutes. This one was a little bit odd because instead of it typical yellowish-orange color, this one was more reddish-orange. It moved very slowly going in a southwestward direction and then suddenly disappeared, just like someone turning off a light switch. We were able to take a few photos of this one.

The second SL appeared at 9:10 p.m. and was in sight for only fifteen seconds. This one seemed to rise up slowly from a nearby wooded area and once it gained some altitude, it simply disappeared. This one also had a reddish tint to it as well. And as all SLs they are completely silent. We noticed that numerous SLs appeared to "rise up" from a wooded area or field.

April 13, 1978

Greg and I as well as four others returned to the field near the Old Prison Camp a few minutes after sunset. The sky was completely void of clouds and the air was still. A half-moon provided some night-time illumination. On this night we spotted two SLs and the first one appeared 8:35 p.m. and was in sight for five minutes. It moved very fast towards the west and was higher than usual. It had this strange reddish tint and it kept on flying until we lost sight of it.

The second SL appeared at 9:00 p.m. and was in sight for five minutes. It appeared just a few degrees above the horizon and moved very slowly in a west to east direction. It stopped once and hovered for about a minute and then resumed it course. This one did not have the odd reddish tint and was bright yellowish-orange.

April 16, 1978

Greg and I along with a friend returned again to the field near the Old Prison Camp. The sky was partly cloudy and there was a ¾ moon to help brighten the night. We saw just one SL this night and it appeared at 9:29 p.m. and it was in sight for two minutes. It was moving low – through an open field towards a wooded area. When the SL went behind the trees, we lost sight of it and it never emerged from the wooded area. This one also had a very noticeable reddish tint.

May 19, 1978

Greg and I along with four friends returned to the field near the Old Prison Camp. This particular field is very large and is situated several feet higher than the actual camp. The sky was partly cloudy and the night air was still. We could on occasion see an almost full moon peeking through the clouds. On this night we spotted one SL and it appeared to our northwest at 9:40 p.m. in the distance and it was much higher from the ground than normal. It did not disappear but slowly drifted out of sight. This one also had that odd reddish tint.

July 17, 1978

Greg and I with a friend were again back at the field near the old prison camp. The sky was clear and a full moon offered its light. There was no wind and the night was hot and humid. We saw one SL and it appeared behind some trees at the edge of a grassy field at 9:49 p.m. and it was in sight for six minutes. This SL moved at a constant slow speed in a west to east direction and was seen until it eventually had moved too far away.

September 24, 1978

Greg and I with a friend returned to the field near the old prison camp. The night sky was clear and there was a slight breeze from the northwest. We spotted one SL this night and it appeared at 9:40 p.m. It moved slow and was in sight for a full six minutes. The luminous orb was flying very high and moving eastward at a faster than normal rate of speed. After a few minutes, it had flown out of sight.

November 01, 1978

I went to SLSA1 and set up my camera on the north end of a large grassy field which was about ¼ mile from the Tenn./Ala. State line. There a few high altitude clouds and the evening air was still. I arrived about thirty-minutes before dark. At 5:54 a bright orange SL suddenly appeared to the west and was moving slowly towards the east. It was possibly about 300-500 feet from the ground and was slowly gaining altitude to maybe 1,000 feet. After watching it for about one minute, the SL had reached its "cruising altitude" and continued flying east until it moved too far away from me to see. This SL was in sight for about six four minutes.

November 12, 1978

I was at SLSA1 this night because of several recent and good SLs sightings (actually I had seen one SL just two days earlier). I arrived just as the sun was setting. The sky was totally clear and the moon was in the west. At 5:50 p.m. a very bright orange SL appeared in the distance to my west. I'm not sure if it suddenly appeared or if it had been traveling and had now came within my view. I'm guessing it was about 600 feet above the ground and it was moving fairly slow. It did not pulsate (that I could see) nor did it, change speed, hover, etc. It kept moving to the east until it was too far away to see it. With my Pentax camera, I managed to take a few good time exposure photos. This SL was in sight for about five minutes. No other SLs were seen that night.

December 02, 1978

I was at SLSA1 a few minutes before dark with a Pentax camera mounted on a tripod. There had many good sightings at this location and I had wanted to get some good photos of a SL that sometimes appeared at dusk. At 5:40 p.m. I noticed a typical CSL1 to the west and it was moving slow to the east. At first I guessed that it was about 500 feet from the ground and was gaining altitude. The SL leveled out at maybe 1000 feet and its speed remained constant. It continued moving eastward and was in sight for about four minutes. Thankfully, I was able to take several photos of this SL.

December 25 1978

Greg (I know, its Christmas night!) was anxious to try out a new pair of binoculars he received earlier that day as a gift so he went to the nearest sighting area. At 8:40 p.m. he spotted a bright but distant SL to the north flying fairly low. Its speed was slow and did not change and it was in sight for several minutes.

January 09, 1979

Greg went to SLSA2 shortly after dark and saw one fairly early in the night. A bright orange orb appeared at 5:50 p.m. and was moving slowly towards the southeast. It moved slowly and through his binoculars Greg noticed that it was not entirely round, and that the left side was much brighter than its right side. This one did not disappear but finally flew out of sight.

January 10, 1979

Greg returned to the same field he was in the night before. It was dark and there was a full moon to illuminate the cloudless sky. At 6:00 p.m. he noticed a very bright SL appear out of the west and was moving fairly fast. After watching the SL for about a minute, it suddenly became dimmer. While the orb was in sight for about four minutes, it remained about 40 degrees above the horizon.

March 05, 1979

Another bright orange SL was seen (by Greg) at SLSA2 at 6:48 p.m. It appeared about ½ mile away and was about 35 degrees above the horizon. The sky was completely void of clouds and a half-moon was rising off the horizon. The night air was cold and there was a slight breeze. The bright orb was moving towards the southeast when it suddenly stopped and was completely still. Then suddenly, it simply disappeared and was not seen again.

February 27, 1979

At SLSA2 another bright orange SL was seen at 6:35 p.m. moving towards the south. Just as this orb was about to be too far away to view it, another bright SL appeared and was moving towards the east. They were both flying low but were not very close. The second SL disappeared for a few seconds and then reappeared and continued its course until it was too far away to be seen.

March 27, 1979

Greg was at SLSA2 by himself on this clear and windless night. The stars were shining and a one-quarter moon could be seen. At exactly 7:00 p.m. a bright orange SL appeared in the east about 30 degrees off the horizon. It was about 1/3 mile away. Two minutes later, the SL flew behind a few trees and apparently disappeared.

July 04, 1979

Greg and his parents along with his sister and brother-in-law were at SLSA2 to hopefully catch a glimpse of a SL on this special holiday. While there was no wind, the sky was partly cloudy. The night air was of course hot and humid. But at 7:13 p.m. their patience was rewarded when a bright orange orb was noticed in the north moving eastward. While it was about ¼ mile away, it was at a higher than normal altitude and was in sight for about three minutes before out of sight.

*Hey! Why watch fireworks when you can watch Spooklights!

July 05, 1979

Greg returned to SLSA2 by himself with the idea to see another SL and hopefully one nearby and at a low altitude. The weather was similar as it was the day before. At 9:15 p.m. he noticed an orange SL in the same flight path as the one he and his family had seen the previous night. With binoculars, Greg was able to watch the SL for about five minutes before it was too far away.

July 23, 1979

Greg and I were back at the field near the old prison camp. The night sky was clear and dark since the moon had not yet risen. The night was hot with no breeze to remove the effects of the summer heat and humidity. On this night Greg and I spotted two SLs with the first one appearing in the sky at about 55 degrees above the horizon in our northwest. Unfortunately, it was farther away than we had hoped. The bright orange orb suddenly appeared and then suddenly disappeared thirty seconds later.

The second SL appeared at 10:00 p.m. and was in sight for two minutes. This one appeared to be about ¾ mile away and was very low –just above some trees. It moved slowly to the southeast and we lost track of it because of the distant trees blocking our view.

July 26, 1979

I went to SLSA1 by myself right before dusk with the idea of trying to observe an early SL and then later meet up with Greg in a field near the Old Prison Camp. At 5:52 p.m. I actually observed two SLs in the sky at the same time. They both used the same flight path, while one was moving towards the west and the other towards the east. They moved very slow and were also very high and the total viewing time was about five minutes.

Later that night, Greg and I drove to a field near the old prison camp. High above us were some scattered clouds with a ¼ moon peeking through. There was a slight breeze but the humidity remained very high. We observed two large SLs that night and the first one appeared at 9:20 p.m. and was visible for just a few seconds as it traveled westward.

The second one appeared at 10:00 p.m. and was in sight for three minutes. It appeared fairly high in the sky at a 60 degree angle and moved toward the southeast. It was a typical Spooklight being about eight feet in diameter and bright orange.

We returned to the old prison camp area the next two nights. Unfortunately, we did not see any SLs.

August 04, 1979

Greg and I returned to the Old Prison Camp area and set up our camera equipment. Actually Greg arrived about thirty minutes before I did and caught sight of an orange SL high in the sky which moved towards the south. It was in sight for less than a minute and then it simply "went out."

The sky was riddled with clouds and there was a slight breeze. The moon could be seen often through the thin cloud cover. We spotted just one SL and it was in sight for just 15 seconds. It appeared at 9:33 p.m. and was moving towards the south. We are not sure if it disappeared or simply went behind some low altitude clouds.

September 28, 1979

One of my best sightings. Please see "The Meeting Of The Two"

October 20, 1979

Greg and I with a mutual friend are back at the OPCA. We arrived just shortly after sunset and began watching the star filled sky. We were beginning to think this would be another "no show" night. But at 10:05 p.m. we observed a bright orange glowing orb moving from the southeast to the northwest at a very high altitude. In fact, it was much higher than normal. Its speed and brightness remained constant as it moved across the sky. This SL was in sight for about three minutes before moving out of sight.

October 25, 1979

Greg and I arrived at SLSA1 shortly after dark and setup our camera. The evening was slightly cool due to a brisk wind. The sky was littered with scattered clouds and there was a full moon shining down on us. We were having some good sightings at this location and wanted to get some photographs.

At 10:02 p.m. we noticed a bright yellowish-orange SL in the distance and it was moving towards the southeast. After watching it for two minutes, it simply vanished.

October 28, 1979

We returned again to SLSA1 at 8:30 and setup our camera. The sky was completely clear and the moon was out. The night air was still and pleasant. Our first sighting was at 9:15 p.m. The SL was typical and was about ½ mile away. It was about 200 feet from the ground and moved slowly until it was out of sight.

At 10:06 p.m. we spotted another slow moving SL at a low altitude about ½ a mile away. It just suddenly appeared and began moving towards the southeast. The orb slowly gained altitude in a weird manner. It looked like it was climbing large steps. This stepping action was very noticeable and this SL is the only one we have ever seen did this type of maneuver. As the SL was "climbing steps" its brightness significantly increased.

Four minutes after it appeared, the glowing ball of light began to "blink" and then suddenly disappeared.

November 01, 1979

Greg and I arrived just before dark at one of our most productive areas; about 1/3 of a mile behind the OPC at the highest point in the large field. A full moon was out and there were some scattered clouds dotting the sky. We made a small camp fire because the night air was very cool. Our camera is ready and we begin watching the sky. It was a long wait because it is not until 10:02 p.m. before we spotted our first SL. It was first noticed to the west and was very low to the ground. It was large and very bright and was moving fast towards the south. It was in sight for two minutes.

The next SL appeared eight minutes later and was barely above some trees to our west. At first, it just hung in the air, illuminating an area with its bright orange light. It was very low to the ground and as it moved eastward, it increased its brightness, speed and altitude. The SL continued on its path and finally after six minutes it had left our visual range.

November 05, 1979

A friend of ours agreed to watch for SLs near SLSA2 and reported he observed a very bright orange SL at 7:30 p.m. moving slowly to the east. It was typical and was in sight for about four minutes.

November 15, 1979

Greg and I (and my younger sister) had became aware of another spot where CSLs could be seen about a few miles northwest from the OPCA, which was about one mile from the Tennessee state line on highway 17. We chose a high spot at the edge of a large field where the SLs had been seen shortly before sunset. We were very interested in this site because the SLs were being observed much earlier than most of the ones at the OPCA.

Just as daylight was yielding to the night, we observed two SLs and both were about eight feet in diameter and were bright orange. The first one suddenly appeared to our west and slowly traveled eastward. We estimated its altitude to be fairly high, perhaps as high as 1500 feet. Fortunately, we had a camera mounted on a tripod and were able to take a few time exposure photos using 400 speed B&W film. This SL was in sight for about five minutes.

The second SL appeared at 5:40 p.m., immediately after the first one had gone out of sight. We began snapping time exposure photos of this one as well. Its appearance and behavior was identical to those of other SL. This included its altitude and speed. The only thing we noticed that was different about the second SL was that when we had our film developed, we noticed that the second SL appeared to be slightly smaller than the first because of the "bright line" from the time exposure of the second SL was smaller than the first one.

November 26, 1979

Greg and I returned to SLSA2 earlier than normal and set up our camera and made a small but necessary camp fire. The sky was clear and there was a full moon in low the sky. We began scanning the sky and at 6:02 p.m. a SL suddenly appeared to the south of us and was slowly traveling in a northeasterly direction. It appeared low- just above some trees not very far away from us and it began to rise to perhaps 1,000 feet. Within six minutes the SL had floated out of sight. Thankfully, we were able to take six time- exposure photos with our tripod mounted Pentax camera.

December 20, 1979

Greg and I were back at the OPCA and as usual, and we chose the highest part of the large field we normally use. We built a much needed camp fire and setup our camera and began to watch the clear and dark sky. At 6:09 p.m. we spotted a bright orange SL moving slowly from the west just above the treetops. It continued moving slowly and was out of our viewing range three minutes later.

At 6:59 another SL appeared near the spot where the first one appeared. Initially, this one moved much slower than the other one and gradually gained altitude. As it moved farther from the ground, it became brighter. It was orange and about eight feet in diameter. We guessed that it finally reached a height of about 2,500 feet. As the SL increased its altitude, it also increased its speed. This SL was in sight for about five minutes.

We attempted to film these two SLs with a Vivitar Super 8 mm movie camera with a 10-power telephoto lens. Unfortunately, we were not successful in videoing the SL because we were not using film not designed for low lighting conditions.

January 23, 1980

Greg went to SLSA2 by himself with the idea of documenting everything he saw in the sky that he deemed noteworthy. Not just Spooklights. He basically wanted to make a record showing how "active" the night sky was.

Here is what Greg's recorded

Time	Type Craft	Direction	Description
6:12	airplane	E-W	- -
6:15	meteor	oh	longest
I've seen			

6:20 - 6:24 (hovering object #2)	*UFO	E-W (n)	#1
6:24	jet	E-W	- -
6:25 crossed over plane	airplane	SE-NW	UFO #3
6:26-6:29	*UFO	SW-NE	#3
6:30- 6:34	*UFO	SW-NE	#4
6:37	airplane	S-N	- -
6:40	jet	N-S	- -
6:47 boom	- -	W	heard
20 sec. later 5-8 seconds	giant orange ball	W	lasted
6:50	airplane	E-W	- -

6:58	airplane	NW-SE	- -
7:02	meteor	oh	- -
7:50	meteor	oh	- -
7:54	airplane	NW-SW	
7:56	airplane	SW-NE	
7:57	airplane	SW-NE	
8:05	left area		

In his journal, Greg recorded:

"UFO #1 was a bright orange ball moving slowly E-W. IT flew over another object that was hovering (UFO #2) which later went out at 6:35. Then UFO #1 blinked on and off three times before finally remaining out completely.

UFO #3 appeared to cross the top of an airplane. When they were both out of sight another UFO, number #4 flew over the same course as UFO #3 had flown. At the same time a jet flew over overhead.

When this was all over I heard a loud boom. About twenty seconds later, I saw a giant orange ball appear, not rise above the treetops to the west of me. It was visible for 5-8 seconds and then went out."

This was a strange night for Greg! Two meteors, a mysterious boom and a giant orange ball (I have no idea what that was!). I wish I had been there!

*During this time, Greg and I some times called the Spooklights UFOs.

January 24, 1980

In all our sightings of the Cloverdale Spooklights up to this time, the events of this night were nothing short of being totally remarkable. This night Greg and I were at the OPCA and we observed a total of seven SLs From 6:15 p.m. to 10:11 p.m. and this did not include the seventeen planes and jets we saw!

All the Spooklights were all bright orange and about eight feet in diameter, but they did not all behave the same. The first SL we noticed (of course I say noticed because we don't always observed the orb approaching us from a distance- they just appear) was to our north and was moving on a west to east path. In fact it was approaching us and we guessed the glowing sphere was at an altitude of about 1,500 feet. After watching the SL for about two minutes, it simply "went out" and was not seen again. It was just as it were a light bulb that was suddenly extinguished when the electricity was turned off. Thankfully, we did take a few photos of this one.

The second SL appeared at 6:45 p.m. and was floating towards the northwest. Actually, it is hard to state with certainty that they are really floating. I suspect they are either being pulled or they possess some type of magnetic energy that serves as a propulsion system. It was moving slowly with an altitude similar to the first SL. This one appeared directly over Greg and me and traversed the sky and eventually was out of sight. It moved slowly and was in sight for about ten minutes. The odd thing about this SL was that while it was moving across the sky it began to oscillate in a very fast and erratic fashion. This is the first time we had ever seen a SL exhibit this behavior. It was as thought the SL had become "unbalanced." We were able to take several photos of this SL.

The next SL appeared at 8:11 p.m. and was in sight for about eleven minutes. This one came out of the southeast and flew very slow to the northwest and it was very low on the horizon. Besides the oscillating characteristics and length of time in sight, it appeared to be a typical SL. As to why this SL acted erratic, we don't know. There was not a strong breeze that night to possibly affect its flight.

The other SLs were typical in size and behavior and did nothing unusual. They were all bright orange and were about eight feet in diameter. We were able to take a total of 22 time exposure photos that night. We would have had more but we decided to make another attempt with a movie camera but were not successful.

February 12, 1980

Greg and I are back at the OPCA just before sunset and built a camp fire and setup our tripod mounted Pentax camera. We were at the same spot where we had observed the seven SLs earlier. At 10:14 we spotted a bright orange SL to the south of us behind some trees in the distance. We guessed the trees were about ½ mile away. It began moving eastward and then turned to the southeast. We once again attempted (again without success) to use a Vivitar movie camera (the camera was fine – the problem was the low speed film) to record this SL. This glowing orb moved fairly slow and was in sight for six minutes.

February 13, 1980

Greg decided to be a loner and look for SLs at SLSA2 and began watching the skies as the sun was dropping below the horizon. The sky was partly cloudy and there was a slight breeze. His wait was long but his patience was rewarded. At 10:09 a bright orange SL appeared moving NW-SW and was to his south. It moved rapidly and was in sight for about one minute. It was fairly low and some distant trees obstructed his view.

Another bright orange SL appeared in the same spot as the first one, only slightly higher in elevation. It traveled the same path as the other and was in sight for about four minutes before being too far away.

March 02, 1980

On this Sunday night, Greg and his father were returning from church (they were near SLSA2) and they noticed an orange SL at 7:10 p.m. moving towards the west at a fairly high altitude. It was bright and moved at a slow rate of speed. After watching the orb for about four minutes, it suddenly disappeared.

March 06, 1980

Greg and I were in a different field but still within a couple of miles from the OPCA. We knew if the SLs could be seen there they should be seen in this area as well. We were at the edge of a very large open field which was near several other smaller fields. The area was flat and our viewing area was quite large.

We sighted a typical CSL1 at 7:02 p.m. in our south and it was moving east to west at treetop level. The SL began to rise slowly and began gaining altitude. But after three minutes, it suddenly disappeared. I suspect that it continued on its course but was not producing visible light.

Another SL appeared at 8:55 p.m. appeared to our south and was moving to the west. It was moving faster than the first one and flew out of sight in about three minutes. We were able to take a few time exposure photos of them.

At 9:01 p.m. a third and final SL appeared just above the ground behind a small group of trees. It slowly gained an altitude of about 300 feet and after a few moments, it disappeared.

March 10, 1980

Greg went to SLSA2 by himself for a couple of hours to scan the skies since the weather was decent and the sky was clear. At 9:14 p.m. he spotted a typical orange SL appeared in the south and was moving towards the east. With his binoculars, he thought he saw a small red orb right beside it (we later learned they may be related). The SL slowly drifted out of sight.

March 14, 1980

Greg and I returned to SLSA2 since we were having some good sightings there. Greg arrived first and started a camp fire. The nighttime air was cold and damp. The sky was clear and a one-half moon was seen to our east. At 8:20 p.m. a bright orange SL appeared to our south and was moving to the west. It was flying very low and was in sight for only a few seconds because some trees blocked our view. At 10:29 another SL appeared moving slowly to the southeast. This orb was a fair distance from us but remained in sight for about seven minutes. During this sighting we noticed a jet overhead flying eastward.

March 18, 1980

We were back at the OPCA in the large field we normally use. The sky was clear with only the stars to provide some nighttime light. The air was cool so we built a camp fire. We had our Pentax camera on a tripod and as always we used a shutter release cable to minimize camera movement when taking photos. We arrived shortly after sunset and began to scan the sky.

We spotted a bright orange SL at 8:22 p.m. and it was almost directly overhead Greg and I and was moving towards the east. It was moving very slowly and was in sight for about fourteen minutes. After about ten minutes of observing this SL we noticed an airplane in the distance. As it came closer to us, we were able to take a time exposure photo of both the airplane and the SL. This is the first time we have been able to do this.

Another SL appeared at 9:44 and flew approximately the same course as the previous SL and was in sight for about two minutes. This SL acted very strangely as it continuously appeared and disappeared. This is one of the reasons Greg and I suspect that there may be many SLs in the area, but only a few are visible. With the necessary magnetic field detection equipment, this theory could possibly be verified (or shot down!).

The third and final SL appeared at 10:09 p.m. and was in sight for about eight minutes. It appeared to the south of us, coming from the west and moving to the east. We were able to take a few time exposure photos of this SL.

April 07, 1980

"John" whom Greg and I have known for a few years reported watching a bright orange SL near SLSA1. "Alan" (another mutual friend) reported watching a bright SL fly over the Old Prison Camp. Unfortunately, we were only given a brief report.

April 08, 1980

After receiving a report from a local high school senior that strange glowing objects had been seen near a different area than where Greg and I normally use, we were able to determine that this field was in the "path" of the other SLs we had seen in the field with "John." We were very curious about this report so we wanted to check out this field. Greg and arrived at this field about a half-hour before sunset and had our tripod mounted camera ready. At 7:09 p.m. we spotted a bright orange SL to our south and began moving to the northwest. It was not very close to us and we guessed the orb was about ¾ of a mile away and reached an altitude of 500 feet. It started moving slowly but after a few moments its speed increased dramatically. The SL was in sight for about six minutes and we had a good opportunity to take some photos.

Another SL appeared at 8:00 p.m. to our south and was moving to the west. It was farther away and moved faster than the previous one. It was in sight for about seven minutes. I'm guessing it was moving at a slightly higher elevation than the other SL.

April 16, 1980

Greg and I arrived at the edge of a large grassy field at about 7:30 p.m. This field is adjacent to Church Road and is about four miles east of Highway 17.   The sky was clear and the air was still. The temperature was normal for this time of year. We used this particular location on and off for about two years and have logged several good sightings.   There was nothing unusual about this viewing site. There are no train tracks or high voltage power lines nearby.

On this night we saw our first Spooklight at 8:39 p.m. It was a typical large bright yellowish-orange orb but it seemed to move faster than normal. It moved in a south to north direction and was in sight for about four minutes.   As soon as this Spooklight had moved out of sight, another one appeared and was similar in size and color as to the other one. This SL flew southeastwardly fairly slow. I estimate the altitude to have been 500 feet or so. It was in sight for five minutes.

The third and last SL seen that night appeared two minutes after the second one had moved out of sight. It was about eight feet in diameter and was bright orange. This one appeared in the south flying over the treetops moving toward the southwest.

April 18, 1980

Greg and I went to the spot where "John" observed a bright SL a few nights earlier. We arrived shortly after dark. The sky was partly cloudy and there was a slight breeze. At 7:19 we all three spotted a bright orange SL appear and flew directly over us. It was moving at a slow (when first spotted) rate of speed and was heading west. It was fairly high in the sky and shortly after we spotted it, the orb began to accelerate and was out of sight at 7:25 p.m.

April 16, 1980

Greg and I arrived at SLSA2 shortly after dark. The sky was clear and a crescent moon was setting in the west. At 8:39 p.m. a bright SL suddenly appeared in the north and flew to the east. It moved very fast and was in sight for just a few moments. Another bright SL appeared at 8:44 p.m. and it flew to towards the southeast. It was fairly high but bright. It was in sight for about five minutes.

Two minutes later another bright orange SL appeared in the south and moved NE-SW. If was flying over the tree tops about a ½ mile away and was in sight for about five minutes.

April 21, 1980

Greg and I are back at the location near the large field adjacent to Church Road. The sky was completely clear of clouds and there the moon was ½ full. On this night we saw only one Spooklight and it appeared at 8:50 p.m. and was in sight for four minutes. It was moving eastwardly at its typical slow speed. We were able to take several photos of this SL using 400 speed film.

April 23, 1980

On this night Greg and I with a friend were at the edge of a large field at a location about two miles west of the location mentioned above. The sky was hazy and the moon was visible. On this night we observed three typical SLs and the first one was spotted at 8:20 p.m. This one just suddenly appeared in the west and we watched it for about twenty seconds and then it suddenly disappeared.

The second SL appeared at 8:51 p.m. and was in sight for four minutes. It flew in a west to east direction and was moving faster than normal. We were able to take a few photos of it.

The third SL appeared at 10:18 p.m. and was in sight for just ten seconds. It suddenly appeared and disappeared. What was strange was that it was not hovering but moving to the south of us, as though it was perhaps there floating in the sky and for some reason became visible for a brief time.

May 20, 1980

On this night Greg and I go back to the other field adjacent to Church Road. The sky was clear and there was a half-moon in the sky. On this night we spotted three bright yellowish-orange orbs and they were all of typical size. The first one is seen at 8:47 p.m. (You may be noticing a pattern to the spring time sightings) and was in sight for three minutes. This one flew directly over us traveling towards the southeast at a fairly high altitude and at a higher than normal rate of speed. We were able to take a few photos of it.

The second SL appeared at 9:02 p.m. and was in sight for four minutes. This one was unusual in that it we thought we could barely see a much dimmer secondary light attached to it. Only until recently did Greg and I actually learn that many do have a secondary light, sometimes it is not seen by the naked eye, but is evident when on video tape.

The third SL appeared at 10:09 p.m. and was in sight for just one minute. It appeared in the north and was moving slowly to the south. We were able to take a few photos of this one.

June 15, 1980

Greg and I are back at the field adjacent to Church Road and on this night we spotted two typical SLs. The first one appeared at 9:13 p.m. and was in sight for three minutes. It was brighter than normal and it flew directly over us traveling westward. The second SL appeared at 9:38 p.m. and was in sight for four minutes. It was flying towards the East and was moving quite fast.

June 19, 1980

Greg and I met at a large field just east of Highway 17 (on CR 24) where we have seen several SLs in the past. We arrived just before dark and setup a tripod mounted camera. The sky was clear and the night was warm and humid. There is no moon to help light up the sky, nor is the air stirring. At 8:54 p.m. we spotted a bright orange SL directly above us and it was very high – and fast. We are not sure if the SL had been moving high above us or if we noticed just as it became visible; for we only observed it for a mere forty-five seconds. This was the only SL we saw that night.

July 01, 1980

Greg and I returned to the above location about an hour before sunset. The sky was filled with high clouds and there is a slight breeze. We had our camera ready. At 8:26 p.m. we noticed a bright orange SL over some trees at the end of the large field we are near. It moved slowly but disappeared one minute later. We are not sure if it really "went out" or if the trees obstructed our view. This was the only SL we saw that night.

July 04, 1980

Greg and I actually included watching for Spooklights as part of our Fourth of July celebration! Like I said, this stuff is addictive! We spotted another one of those mysterious white orbs that night and it appeared at 9:15 p.m. out of the north and was moving to the south. It appeared smaller than the typical bright orange SL and was moving very fast. This white orb was in sight for two minutes. We did not see any typical SLs that night.

We were beginning to wonder how many kinds of Spooklights exist and possibly most (or at least some) of them either not visible to the human eye, are possibly the move so fast they are difficult to spot.

July 17, 1980

Greg and I returned to the 04 July location and we arrived well before dark. The sky was clear and the moon is ½ full. There is also a slight but humid breeze out of the south. At 8:25 p.m. we noticed a small white glowing orb very high in the sky and moving very fast in a southwardly direction. It was in sight for one minute. The white light contained no blinking lights and no sound was heard.

As soon as the white orb vanished, Greg and I spotted a typical orange SL to our north and it was moving slowly towards the east. It flew out of sight within two minutes. We learned over the years that when a non typical Spooklight is seen, most likely a typical SL will soon appear (there have been exceptions). No need to ask me why. I don't know!

At 10:27 p.m. we observed another orange SL to our north but this one was traveling in a south east direction. It was almost out of sight when we spotted it and was in view for only thirty seconds.

July 26, 1980

Greg and I are back to our June 19 location and we arrived several minutes before darkness came. The sky was cloudy and the night air was warm. At 9:15 p.m. we spotted a small white orb moving very fast towards the south. We have heard of a few reports of fast moving white orbs but had not seen any of them ourselves – until now. It was not a plane for there were not blinking lights, no sound or other characteristics that would be associated with an airplane. We really don't know what this white orb was. Unfortunately, not photos were taken.

July 29, 1980

Greg and I are back to the above location and arrived about an hour before dark. The sky was clear and we knew the moon be in view later in the night. We spotted the first of two SLs at 8:52 p.m. and it was about forty degrees off our northern horizon. It continued moving northeast at a moderate speed until it was too far away to be seen. This SL was in sight for two minutes. The second and final SL for the night appeared at 9:58 p.m. and it was directly above us. Within a few seconds of watching this orange orb, it simply "went out."

July 30, 1980

Greg and I went back to the same place as the night before. As usual, we arrived early and set up our camera. The sky was littered with high clouds and the moon was scheduled to rise shortly after 10:00 p.m. At 8:58 p.m. we both noticed another one of those white orbs moving northeasterly. The object was only in sight for about thirty seconds which made it difficult to learn much about it.

At 9:01 p.m. another (or was it?) small white orb appeared and we noticed that it was flying directly overhead and it was moving towards the north. It was rather small and was moving fast. After watching it for about one minute, it also "went out."

At 9:08 p.m. we spotted a large and very bright orange SL north of us and it was moving very slowly towards the east. It was high in the sky and did not change its speed or elevation. This SL continued moving slowly for about five minutes until it was out of sight. Thankfully, we were able to take some photos.

Five minutes later, we spotted another (or was it the same?) bright orange SL moving much faster than the other one towards the southeast. While it was in sight for about two minutes, we were able to take some photos.

A bright orange SL was seen at 10:27 p.m. and also was flying directly overhead of us. This one had a different flight path and was moving in a southeasterly direction. This one also "went out" after viewing it for about thirty seconds.

We realized that somehow the white orbs are associated to the larger orange SLs, but we are not sure how. Nor do we know why the white orbs generally travel faster than the orange ones.

\

August 21, 1980

Greg and I are back to the above spot again and even though it has been a few weeks since our last sightings we wanted to try this place again. When the sun had gone below the horizon we had a half moon hanging in the sky which offered a small amount of illumination. There were no clouds and no breeze. The night was hot and humid. At 8:25 p.m. we noticed a very bright orange SL to our south and it was moving towards the west. We guessed it was about a mile away from us but the view was very good. We were able to take several photos of this bright orb. It continued to mover slow and was in sight for seven minutes.

Four minutes later we spotted another bright orange SL to our north and this one was very low – just over some trees in the distance. This one would move slowly and then stop and hover for several seconds before moving again. We also took some photos of this one too.

November 02, 1980

Greg and I were stationed at a large open grassy field a couple of miles southeast of the OPC. The sky was clear and the night air was cool. We had one sighting that night. A typical bright orange SL appeared to our west at 11:15 p.m. It was possibly ¾ of a mile west of us and was traveling eastward. It was fairly high in the clear sky and moved very slowly. It was in sight for about five minutes.

November 03, 1980

We were back at SLSA1 and had arrived at about 5:15 p.m. The sky was clear and the night was cool. At 5:58 p.m. we noticed a typical SL to our south and it was moving towards the Northeast. The SL was only in sight for fifteen seconds before doing its famous vanishing act.

At 9:32 p.m. another orange SL appeared to our south and it was moving eastward at a slow rate of speed. It was fairly high in the sky and was an "unusual" Spooklight. It was in sight for four minutes before we lost sight of it.

November 07, 1980

Greg and I returned to the same spot as the above location hoping to get a better SL sighting than we did a week earlier. The sky was clear and the night was cool. This night turned out to be one of our best nights ever! We spotted eight SLs from 5:58 p.m. to 8:33 p.m. And we were able to take several photos of these SLs.

The first one appeared in the east and flew rapidly in a southwest to northeast direction. It had flown out of sight within three minutes. At 6:35 p.m. we noticed that a large bright orange SL suddenly appeared a feet above some nearby trees. It was moving very slowly and after observing it for about thirty seconds, it suddenly vanished.

One minute later another SL appeared in the east and flew south – just above the tree tops and then it suddenly vanished. As soon as this one disappeared, another one appeared (or was it the same SL?) in the same area but at a higher elevation and flew out of sight within three minutes.

At 7:25 p.m. we noticed a large SL hovering in the west – it was very low to the ground and maybe a 1/3 of a mile away. It began moving very slowly and within a minute it had went behind some trees in the distance and was no longer in view. At 8:30 p.m. we spotted another (or was it the same?) SL hovering about 100 feet from the ground, but much farther away. This one too, suddenly disappeared and was in view for less than one minute.

November 11, 1980

On this night we wanted to be SLSA1 and we arrived at about 5:00 p.m. The sky was totally void of any clouds and there was a slight breeze from the south. At 7:09 p.m. we noticed a brighter than normal SL appeared in the south traveling an east to west direction at a very slow speed. Its altitude was perhaps 600 feet and was in sight for about seven minutes.

November 20, 1980

Greg and I returned to the above location and this time the night is cool and the sky is filled with high altitude cirrus clouds. There is a full moon in the sky but no wind. At 6:53 p.m. we spotted a large bright orange SL moving to the north and it is very slow and low to the ground. It was difficult to keep track of it as it is behind some trees but we watch it move slowly across a large field. After about ten minutes, it was too far away for us to view it.   At 7:14 p.m. we noticed another large orange SL to the south of us. It was moving very slow towards the west. This one was maybe 500 feet from the ground and we had an excellent view of this wondrous orb. We were able to view it for almost eight minutes before it was too far way.

At 9:55 p.m. another orange SL was seen high in the sky traveling in a NW-SE direction.   This orb moved very slowly and then it suddenly vanished. This SL was in sight for about nine minutes.

January 21, 1981

A local newspaper ran a front page article about our Spooklight investigations called *Local UFO Investigation Team Gets Saucer Theory Shot Down*. Our basic premise was that many of the nocturnal UFO sightings reported for the last several years in this area were not physical objects of an extra-terrestrial origin but were the result of the earth's natural energies producing bright luminous phenomena. While we stressed there was a natural explanation we also emphasized that the processes involved are complex and poorly understood.

Source: *Florence Times*

June 02 1981

A very odd "fireball" was seen by eight witnesses on 02 June 1981 flying a short distance west of Cloverdale. The ball of fire was very bright as it was seen crossing over highway 20. Shelia Thompson of the Florence Times wrote an excellent article entitled *"Mysterious Fireball Puzzles Authorities."* According to Shelia, "Eyewitnesses said a "ball of fire" that looked like a burning airplane or helicopter crossed Highway 20 about eight miles north of Florence during thunderstorm Tuesday afternoon."

While this sighting is strange and is not as easy to classify as a "normal" Spooklight, I include it in this book because of the location where it was sighted. The "8 miles north of Florence" is in the Spooklight corridor. This area is where a lot of Spooklight have been sighted. Another reason is that the sighting occurred at about 7:30 p.m., which is not an unusual time to spot a large orange glowing orb.

This chapter does not include all of the Spooklights Greg and I have seen. I intentionally excluded more than forty sightings. In particular, I have omitted several sightings were there was only one witness.

I include this June 02, 1981 sighting because it was seen flying in the "path" of the other SLs seen at SLSA4. This sighting could have been an unusual and exceptionally impressive ball lightning sighting since it was seen during a thunderstorm. Or possibly it was a SL that was "different" because of the additional electrical energy in its area.

After the Early Years: From Then To Now

For a period of time, neither Greg nor I was able to devote any significant amount of time to studying the SL phenomenon. Work, school, and being a new husband began to consume my time. I also began to move around a lot because of my employment. Greg had many things going on in his life as well. Our interest in the CSL phenomenon had not dissolved;

but many of our opportunities to continue our sightings did. From 1981 through 1984, Greg and I would plan to watch SLs about two to three times a year. We normally were not disappointed and would continue to view them as we had before.   In 1985 I left the Florence area and began to work in various areas of the country.   Making special trips to Cloverdale was not practical. We did return to SLSA3 about once a year (Greg would go perhaps two to three times a year with a friend) just to see if they could still be seen. These trips were based on my vacation time to visit family members living in Florence. Sometimes we would see the SLs and sometimes we would not. We concluded that this phenomenon was not changing over time.

Beginning in 2001, Greg and I began to talk more seriously about taking up our research again, even if it was going to be on a limited basis. We realized our interest in these SLs had not died over the years; but had merely become dormant. We knew that we had made no real attempt to publicize our research with the hopes of this phenomenon being studied by professional scientists. We began to feel like it was now time to tell our story.

I began to coordinate my trips to Alabama (which is about 370 miles from where I live) with Greg's schedule and would try to spend one nigh at either SLSA3 or SLSA4 when I was in the area visiting my family. Even this year (2006) I made two special trips to Cloverdale with the intent to view and take pictures of the SLs. On my second trip to Cloverdale in 2006, noted author and researcher Brent Raynes was able to be with Greg and me at SLSA4. I had a great time just being with Brent and him sharing some of the interesting things he has seen and learned over the years.

While the majority of the SLs I have seen were in the early years, I have seen several since then. There is no doubt that the Spooklight sighting areas are still very active today.

Time exposure photograph of large Spooklight moving eastward near SLSA2. Photo taken with Pentax camera and 400 speed film.

Directions to the sighting areas:

It is not difficult to find some of the better sighting areas. They are all near public roads so there are no long hikes into the woods or hills. While I encourage others to watch these glowing orbs, I am also aware that most property owners are not eager to have uninvited guests on the land at night. So if you need to use private property, please seek permission first.

Directions to:

SLSA1

To reach this spot drive north (from Florence) on Highway 17 until you are about ½ miles from the Tennessee State line. If you are at the State Line, then the SLs will be seen in the south and they usually travel in a west to east direction. Even though we have seen many SLs here, Greg and I haven't used this site for quite some time. The property we used changed owners a few years ago and I not asked for permission to access the field we used to use.

SLSA2

This area can be accessed by turning east onto Highway 24 while traveling north on Highway 17. Cross over the train tracks and go about one mile. Greg and I have spotted many SLs in this area. While this is an active area, we now prefer either SLSA4 or SLSA3.

SLSA3

This area is what we call the Old Prison Camp area or OPCA because this area includes the prison camp property as well as the large fields which border it. The best way to get to the prison camp is to leave Florence on Highway 17 going north. About five miles from the Tennessee State line is Wilson High School on the left. Less than a mile past the school is CR224 (also called Mt. Zion Road); turn right and cross the railroad tracks and then turn left and follow the road a short distance. There you can either turn right or go straight. If you go straight, the road will end at the entrance gate to the prison camp.

While I have permission to use one of the adjacent fields, the general public does not. What I suggest is that if possible, park at a clearing at the railroad tracks and walk north on the tracks for about ¼ mile. This would place you in an excellent location to view SLs.

SLSA4

This is the location Greg and I have used during the past four years or so. One reason is that this area is very active and the other reason is that we have permission from a land owner to use one of his large fields.

If you are in Florence (that is the town Greg lives in) drive north on Highway 157 a short distance to Cloverdale and then continue north until you intersect with County Road 272. At this point you are only about 3 miles or so to the Tennessee State line. To your right is CR 272. You can either continue driving on Highway 157 or turn right. As the SL travels in its east to west direction, it will cross Highway 157 somewhere in this vicinity. If you turn right and travel up the road you will be a slightly higher elevation and thus will be in a better location. The SL usually travels parallel (to the south) to CR 272.

I am not suggesting these four locations are the only places to watch SLs. There may be better areas to go to. Once you watch a few SLs, you should be able to determine their "path' and use a map and compass to locate other and perhaps better locations.

This is a rough sketch showing the four Spooklight locations Greg and I have found. A few miles due east of SLSA4 is Lexington where several Spooklights were seen in the early 1970s. During the past few years we have been going to SLSA4. This spot is easy to drive to, is active and we have permission from a land owner to use his property. The unused prison camp is located on property that is part of SLSA3.

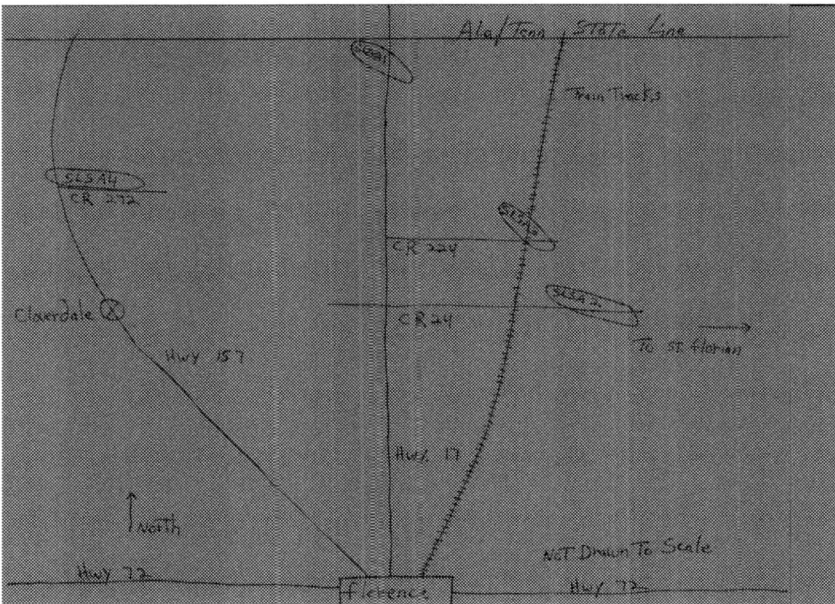

The February 25, 2006 Spooklight Video

Greg and I had planned my trip for several weeks. Our major objective for this trip was to video at least one SL. We had lots of photos of the SLs but no video footage. Since I live in South Carolina it was no small commitment for me. We also needed the weather to be cooperative; for heavy rain, below freezing temperatures and even snow are possible in February. I drove 370 miles and arrived in Florence at about 4:30 p.m. My plan was to spend two nights with Greg at the SLSA4 sighting area. Fortunately for us, the weather forecast was for a cloudless sky with a slight breeze. The down side was that the nighttime temperature would drop to about 32 degrees.

We went out to SLSA4 which is a short distance north of Cloverdale. I wish I could be more specific about the location of the field (about 100 acres), but the owner has for several years generously given us permission to use his field when ever we wanted to – provided that we do not reveal any personal information about the owner – including the owner's name. The owner is well aware of the Spooklights and has watched those dozens of times during the past several years. The owner does not want any publicity nor does the owner want the field to become a tourist site. Fortunately, there are many other fields that would make excellent viewing areas.

The first night which was the 24th, Greg and I arrived before dark and set up two cameras on tripods. The air temperature begin to drop so we made a camp fire near were we keep our lawn chairs. This field connects to another large field so we have a large viewing area to our East and West. We were also situated at the highest part of the field which increased our viewing area. While our hopes were high, for what ever reason, we did not see any Spooklights that night. That in itself was unusual. Greg and I left the viewing area slightly after midnight and determined to return the next night.

The next night I arrived about an hour before dark. Greg arrived a few minutes after sunset. I already had a camp fire and the equipment set up. And then we waited. I had hoped for an early sighting for about 5% of our sightings have been before 6:30 p.m. At about 10:20 p.m. we saw our first and only Spooklight that night. It suddenly appeared hovering about ½ miles away to our south and began to travel slowly eastward which was unusual. They normal travel westward. It was an excellent sighting and the bright Spooklight was in sight for about four minutes. Due to some technical problems with our video camera, we were able to video the Spooklight for slightly more than two minutes.

After viewing the video numerous times, we discovered a tertiary or secondary light attached to the front of the main body of the Spooklight. We learned for the first time there is about a 2 foot long of energy connecting the two orbs. The small orb was not as bright as the main light. We are not really sure if all SLs have this secondary light or not.

We also got a good look at how the orbs pulsate. It was apparent to Greg and I that these Spooklights are spheres comprised of plasmoid energy. The energy seems to be intense and focused enough to produce a visible globe for a few minutes. There was not just one pulse at a time but many small pulsations that appear to be occurring at random. With this type of pulsations, the light seemed to be steady, but was actually quiet the opposite.

I would speculate that when the Spooklight is able to become visible, it becomes either unstable and disappears or the energy becomes more stable and remains visible for some time. This means that SLs are possibly present in the area but nor visible – until the energy is intense enough or focused. The source of this energy is not clearly understood.

Greg and I are available to assist serious Spooklight researchers if interested in actual field sightings of the Cloverdale Spooklights. I can be contacted at:

wyattknows@yahoo.com

Frequently Asked Questions

When is the best time to arrive at a viewing site?

My suggestion is to arrive a few minutes before sunset and be able to remain there until at least 11:00 p.m. One of my best sightings occurred a few minutes after sunset and another one of my best sightings occurred at 10:20 p.m. The latest SL sighting I experienced occurred shortly before midnight.

How many will be seen in one night?

That depends. It depends on the weather (fog, low clouds, etc.), your viewing site (some are better than others), how long you are there, and other factors can determine how many you will seen in one night. One theory suggests that fewer will be seen when there is a thunderstorm in the area because its electrical energy somehow causes interference. In addition some nights are just better than others. Greg and I have spent many nights in our favorite viewing sites and did not observe any SLs. Other nights, Greg and I have seen as many as eight!

What do they look like?

The typical yellowish-orange Type 1SL is about eight feet in diameter (a few seem to be slightly larger) and is very bright. They are silent and somewhat unpredictable. They can suddenly appear and disappear, but never do they change shape or size. They are not a physical object and are not affected by the wind.

The Type 2 SL is about 2-4 feet in diameter and is white. They are rarely seen and are not seen near the ground, as some Type 1 SLs are. They usually move at a higher rate of speed than the Type 1 SLs and have never been seen to stop and hover.

The Type 3 SL is also rarely seen and is about the same size as the Type 2 SL. The Type 3 is a dull bluish color and also moves quiet fast.

Are they somehow related to the other UFO phenomena?

Based on my understanding, these SLs are not related to any UFOs that are physical objects. They have been mistaken for a typical UFO on several occasions, especially during the 1973 UFO flap in Lauderdale County. But since they are not solid objects, I do not believe they are part of the UFO phenomenon in regards to space ships visiting earth.

I will quickly add that they are not "probes" sent out by the "mother ship" seeking to monitor our activities. These SLs travel a predictable "path" and do not display the normal characteristics that are usually assigned to the extraterrestrial based UFOs.

Are they "paranormal" in nature?

Greg and I examined this theory very seriously a number of times as being a possible explanation. We wanted to know if other occult phenomena in the area may be related to these Spooklights. North Alabama seems to have its share of the paranormal activity.

Greg and I spoke with two local and unrelated people who claimed to have been in contact with aliens. We also visited a house that the owners claimed to be haunted (Greg and I are convinced the couple had experienced some type of poltergeist activity. And there were a few other haunted house reports that we aware of. While I realize my personal "data base" is limited, It is clear to me that there was no real direct evidence connecting the "usual" paranormal happenings of the area with the Cloverdale Spooklights.

To be honest this question weighed heavy on our minds for a few years and we actually tried to prove that the Spooklights were a type of paranormal phenomena. They were "paranormal" in one sense, yet we could not find a link between the SLs and the paranormal which would include psychic phenomena, ghosts, etc.

Why aren't they seen during the daytime?

This is a question that both believers and skeptics ask. The answer is, some Spooklights have been seen shortly before sunset. But by and large they are seen either as the sun is setting or after sunset. They are not usually reported during the daytime. There seems to be two possible answers to this question. One, they are there, floating in the corridor just like they are at night with one exception. Somehow the sunlight is acting as a squelching agent that prevents the Spooklight from producing visible light or the sunlight actually acts a squelching agent and prevents the formation of the SLs.

It does seem to Greg and me that sunlight (high amounts of photons) is probably responsible for not observing Spooklights during the daytime.

Why aren't they seen crossing the road or over people's houses?

Actually they do cross over roads and people's houses. They are usually a few hundred feet high when they do. We have never seen any cross over roads at very low altitudes go through a building. Because SLs don't fly very close to people (houses and roads), some researchers suggest that the SLs intentionally "avoids" people. Is it possible they are alive or is it possible our own bioelectrical energy somehow interferes with the energy fields of the SLs?

Is there an intelligence associated with the Spooklights?

Now that is an interesting question! Believe it or not this question has haunted Greg and me for several years. Almost every time Greg talk about Spooklights this subject is brought up. Most of the Spooklights merely float in the air along their path and either go outside our viewing area or simply vanish in plain sight. Some hover and some don't. Does that mean they are intelligently controlled? The answer is no. Yet- the question remains. How do we explain the Spooklight that suddenly appeared directly above some railroad tracks and apparently "waited" on the train to pass under it and then "followed" the train? It did and does seem to us that this Spooklight must have "known" about the coming train or why else would it have not only appeared above the tracks but do so just a few moments before the train arrived? Or was the Spooklight hovering above the tracks for some time, but became visible when it "realized" the train (another energy source or "thought" it was another Spooklight) was approaching? Or I am over analyzing the event?

What about the sighting I had when two Spooklights traveled on the exact flight path and then "merged" (or merely "hooked up") together for a few moments? And then they separated and went their separate ways. Or what about the sighting Greg and I had when a SL "split" into two Spooklights for a few seconds and then regrouped to form what appeared to be one SL? Could it have been two SLs traveling together? And that thought raises many more questions!

I admit that Greg and I are mystified and uneasy about this idea. The very thought that there is some kind of intelligence associated with SLs is almost unnerving. The ramifications boggle my mind (my mind is easy to boggle!). Now the question demands to be asked: Are they alive?

And how could I even pose this question with any hint of seriousness? First of all, I am not saying there is any intelligence associated with these Spooklights. I am unable to offer any real proof that suggests they are alive. But I do at least ask the question. And I am by no means the first person to seriously ponder this thought.

There is an interesting book that was published several years ago called *Sky Creatures: Living UFOs* and was written by Trevor James Constable. According to this author his provocative book"…presents UFOs as they have never been presented before-as biological organisms native to our atmosphere that have been living with us, side by side, unnoticed, since the beginning of time."

I will add that this book was published in 1976 and as far as I know, no direct evidence had been discovered since its publication suggesting there are large spherical self-illuminating bioforms living in our atmosphere. But do we really know?

How long have people being seeing the Spooklights?

The earliest confirmed report that I know of occurred in early 1973 a short distance from Lexington. A woman and her son reported viewing

SLs on a regular basis near St. Florian in 1975. Since the SLs have been seen consistently in the same general area for more than three decades, I assume they have been around for a much longer period of time.

Are they seen anywhere else?

Yes. There are other areas in this "window" or corridor where SLs can be viewed. The window or at least the most active part of the window seems to be about 15 miles long (about five miles wide) beginning just north of Cloverdale and seems to end near Lexington.

Can they be seen without optical aids?

Yes. The observer can be close enough to the SL where optical aids are not required. While the distance from the observer varies, they are very bright and usually easy to spot.

Is it possible to take good photos of the Spooklights?

Yes. I suggest using a good quality camera mounted on a tripod.

What causes them to move or hover?

This is another part of the mystery Greg and I continue to ponder. Some hover and some don't. And for what purpose? The amount of visible light produced does not seem to change while hovering or moving. The SLs are not affected by wind. They have been seen on numerous occasions to float into the wind and their speed seems constant even in a brisk wind.

What causes them to vanish?

These plasmoid orbs constantly pulsate, but their frequency is unknown. It is possible that their pulsation frequency is identical to the frequency of the energy that gives birth to a Spooklight. Or perhaps they produce their own frequencies. One theory is that only at certain frequencies do the SLs produce visible light. They still exist and are traveling in their path, but are not visible.

So when a Spooklight "disappears," it sometimes reappears a few seconds later. Sometimes they do not reappear. But do they still continue exist?

Could there be many invisible SLs and only a few are visible or are they spontaneously produced when the subterranean electromagnetic fields are strong enough? And do they become extinguished once the energy dissipates?

My personal view is that since SLs suddenly appear "out of nowhere" and can suddenly disappear and reappear, that they exist at least for a while before they are visible. It is even possible that they are primarily invisible and only visible for a relatively short period of time. My gut feeling is that for the most part, they are not visible to the human eye.

But with the proper equipment they could be detected even while in their invisible state.

Do the Cloverdale Spooklights interact with people?

Based on more than 180 Spooklights that I have observed, interviews, research (numerous published articles and books about other Spooklights), etc. it seems to me that they are somehow affected by the close proximity of people. I am not aware of anyone coming into direct contact with this type of Spooklight or of anyone getting within fifty feet or so of one. And there are plenty of accounts where unsuccessful attempts have been made to approach a SL. I am not aware of any reports of Spooklights passing through buildings (houses, barns, etc.) or vehicles. Either the SL "avoids" people or possibly reacts with the witness' own bioelectrical field (the human brain does produce electrical energy) and possibly compromises the integrity of the Spooklight or somehow repels it.

Could the head lights of nearby cars or trains be causing these SLs?

No. Unlike the Spooklights in Marfa, Texas or Brown Mountain, North Carolina where this theory has been proposed and accepted by some, this phenomenon is far different! These SLs are seen in plain sight and there is no mirage or reflected lights involved.

Are seasons a factor?

Greg and I observed fewer SLs during the months of June, July and August. Our view is that the months October through April are best for viewing SLs. But I add that while fewer have been seen during the hot summer months, some of the better sightings have occurred during this time.

Does moonlight affect the SLs?

Greg and I have had many excellent sightings with the moon in view and without the moon in view. The moon is not a factor.

What if a SL approaches the observer? Are they dangerous?

While it is highly unlikely that an observer will either approach a SL within a hundred feet or so and equally unlikely that a SL will move close to you, Greg and I are not aware of any evidence that leads us to think they are dangerous. They do not appear to possess any significant amount of thermal energy. However, I will strongly urge caution when dealing with any kind of energy that is not understood.

Is weather a factor?

Fewer SLs will be seen during inclement weather for a number of reasons which include fog, low clouds, electrical storms, intense rain, etc. It is possible that the electrical energy contained in a major storm may interfere with the production of SLs. Also few people are outside during inclement weather.

How long are they visible?

It is not possible to predict how long they will be visible. Some are visible for just a few seconds and some are visible for up to ten minutes. I would guess that on an average, a typical sighting lasts about three minutes.

Are the Cloverdale Spooklights associated with train tracks?

Please read the Spooklights and Train Tracks chapter.

Spooklights and Train Tracks

There is no doubt in my mind that several (not all) Spooklights are seen at or within a short distance from railroad tracks. Some researchers even go so far as to suggest that train tracks are necessary to produce SLs. While I am not in a position to refute what some researchers have proposed, I would add that the types of Spooklights seen at railroad tracks are different than the Cloverdale Spooklights. For example, the Spooklights seen near Gurdon, Arkansas are about 1-2 feet in diameter and perhaps a direct relationship exists between this phenomenon and train tracks. Is it possible that somehow the electrical energy (voltage and electron flow) produced beneath the earth's surface creates powerful pulsating electrical and magnetic fields below and above the earth's surface? Do these pulsating subterranean electrical fields interact with each other and as a result create strong magnetic fields which while pulsating in the presence of many tons of steel, induces fluctuating voltages and currents in the train tracks?

For a neat experiment wrap a length of insulated wire around a large iron nail and then connect the two ends of the wire to a standard 1 ½ volt battery; one to the positive (top side) and one to the negative (bottom side) ends of the battery. When you do this you will have an electromagnet and its magnetic strength may surprise you!

And if there is relative motion between a magnetic field (man made or natural) and an electrical conductor (copper, underground water, aluminum, etc), voltage will be produced and if there is an electrical path, then electron flow (current) will occur.

Another interesting fact about iron (the main ingredient for railroad tracks) is that the subatomic components of the iron atoms use more energy to keep their atoms together than other metals. This means that iron is the most "stable" of all metals. Railroad tracks also contain small amounts of carbon which is also an excellent electrical conductor.

Just like in modern electrical power transformers, an iron core is necessary for the power flowing through the conductors to change from a low to high voltage.

But even if there are strong magnetic fields sometimes created at these railroad tracks, does this somehow produce the Spooklight or perhaps merely attracts them or possibly interacts with a non visible Spooklight and makes it visible?

For me, there is no doubt there is some kind of link between some Spooklights. There are too many reports of glowing orbs seen floating over railroad tracks. While I don't think the CSL sightings at railroad tracks are a coincidence (one of my best Spooklight sightings involve railroad tracks), it seems to me that they play a small role in the Spooklight phenomena. Perhaps the SLs are at times attracted to the magnetic fields surrounding the tracks, or perhaps these magnetic fields interact with the Spooklights and merely cause them to be visible to the human eye. It seems to me that much more research needs to be conducted to prove or disprove these suppositions.

The time exposure photo on the left shows a Spooklight seen at SLSA1. I intentionally closed the camera's shutter as it appeared to intersect with the utility pole.

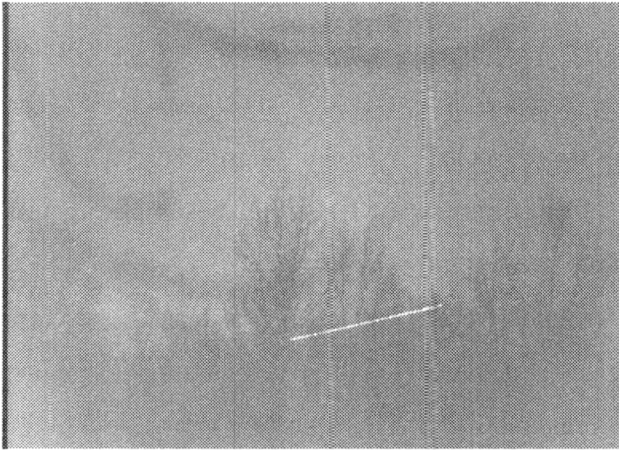

The time exposure on the left shows a large bright Spooklight seen at SLSA3. It is a rising above a large wooded area and moving to the west.

I realize that several excellent Spooklight sightings have been reported near or directly above train tracks and some highly respected researchers have suggested that train tracks are necessary to produce SLs. In fact, years ago, when these glowing orbs were first called Spooklights and some folks believed the small glowing orbs seen floating above train tracks was the spirit of someone who either died when struck by a passing train or the train engineer's ghost is walking the tracks at night with a lantern searching for some one who was killed by his train.

Most Spooklight sightings seem to suggest that the luminous phenomena are fairly small and are about the size of a train engineer's lantern.

One good example is the Spooklight seen in Gurdon, Arkansas where numerous people over the years have claimed to have seen mysterious balls of light floating across some railroad tracks. Other examples abound so the question remains. Is there a relationship or connection between Spooklights and train tracks?

One of my best (I have three that I call my "best") SL sightings involved both a train and train tracks. Another of my best sightings occurred less than a ½ mile from train tracks. My other best sighting was more than three miles from the nearest train tracks.

If a Spooklight Corridor extends from Cloverdale to at least Lexington, then why aren't they being seen in more areas inside this corridor? Most likely there are a number of reasons why there are so few known locations.

First, if railroad tracks are a direct factor, then most sighting areas will be where there are train rails. And if I understand [3]Bearden's theory (additional information below) correctly, underground currents should flow perpendicular to the train rails for the luminous spheres to be formed. Subterranean electrical currents flowing parallel to the rails will not interact with them in the fashion necessary to produce the type of magnetic fields at the needed intensity which will "kindle" or trigger the Spooklight event. And there may be other factors involved, including an

---

[3] In addition to this chapter, please refer to my Explanations chapter for Thomas Bearden's theory on how Spooklights at rail road tracks are formed. I recommend his book, *Excalibur Briefing* which attempts to scientifically explain this phenomenon as well as other types of "paranormal" events. If interested, I suggest visiting his web site: chenier.org.

ample amount of quartz and water. Quartz experiencing geologic stress to produce electrical currents and the water to act as a conductor are both required. Also, there are many areas in this corridor that are largely unpopulated and are covered by dense forests. Even if there were very low altitude Spooklights in an area, they would not be visible to anyone more than a ½ mile away or so. There could be dozens of active Spooklight sighting areas unknown because of these reasons.

Of course, there are SL sightings not connected with train rails. I have seen several of these orange orbs within a half mile of train rails, but I have also seen several more than two miles away from any train tracks.

So for me, my so-called Spooklight Corridor is not dependent upon the magnetic fields produced by train tracks. For one reason, I do not claim the train tracks are really responsible for the formation of the Spooklights. There is an energy source that is responsible and this energy can form SLs with or without train tracks. Perhaps train tracks are not the producer of the orbs but possibly acts as an attractor.

It seems to me that the formation of Spooklights is a very complex phenomenon involving significant amounts of electrical currents and multiple magnetic fields. Other contributing factors may include ambient temperature, atmospheric pressure, and electrical energy that may act as a squelching agent. And I dare not rule out railroad tracks as a contributing factor!

Since there are almost no documented cases (that I know of) where people came close enough to physically interact with a Spooklight, it would seem to me that the idea of electrical fields created by the human brain may act as an extinguishing agent could have merit. The only possible exception would be rare reports of some one getting within touching distance of a Spooklight is when the orb is very small and the person's electrical field would have less effect on it, in contrast to a larger orb.

The Maco Station Spooklights near Wilmington, North Carolina were supposedly reported by thousands of people beginning in the 1860s. The mysterious Spooklight would often appear quiet small and then increase its size until it appeared to be about the size of a lantern. The Spooklights were always seen on a particular section of railroad track.

Maco is located in Brunswick County in the southern section and the sighting area is about 14 miles northwest of Wilmington on the Wilmington-Florence-Augusta line.

According to one website, the Maco Spooklights stopped being reported in 1977 when the railroad tracks were removed. Leave it to those railroad tracks to make things difficult for me!

The fact that the Spooklight sightings ended when the metal rails were removed seem to add significant weight to the idea that magnetized rails play a role in either producing Spooklights or causing them to be visible.

The Surrency Spooklights are a well known phenomenon near Surrency, Georgia where many SL sightings have been reported. The sighting area is a section of the Macon/Brunswick railroad that runs through this small town. These Spooklights have been reported to be bright yellowish in color and their size is less than a foot in diameter. The Gurdon (Arkansas) Spooklight are well known and are also associated with train tracks.

A very interesting hypothesis proposed and expounded by [4]Thomas Bearden to explain Spooklights is in his book, *Excalibur Briefing*. While Bearden is specifically attempting to explain the Morris County, New Jersey mystery lights, he states on page 20 in regarding the train tracks where the Spooklights are seen, "the rails are oriented parallel to the fault line, which means the rock stresses are oriented perpendicular to the rails. Thus the telluric currents piezoelectrically induced by the quartz and other minerals in the local granite are also generally oriented perpendicular to the rails and below them"

He continues with his thoughts and says, "These piezoelectric currents thus constitute effective coils about the rails, magnetizing them weakly along their length, but this is in addition to their normal magnetism, if any picked up due to the specific local and atmospheric electricity changes."

What he seems to be saying is that if the piezoelectric induced currents are perpendicular to the length of the rails, there will be a weak magnetic field on each of the rails. The length of the magnetic field could be fairly short or very long. There is also a third magnetic field which is much

---

[4] Thomas Bearden's is a retired military officer and well known scientist and his website is: cheniere.org. Greg and I had the privilege of meeting him on a few occasions during the late 1970s.

larger and exists above the rails. It encompasses the rails and their individual magnetic fields. The height of the secondary magnetic field would be determined by the subterranean currents. And inside this larger secondary field is where the Spooklight will be produced by the interaction of the three magnetic fields (two from the rails and from the secondary field.

According to this view, the large secondary field encompassing the train rails acts as a "tunnel" for the Spooklight.

According to Bearden, the observer of the phenomena can possibly "generate or extinguish electrostatic, magnetic, and electromagnetic fields at a distance, even through a superconductive faraday shield." Which means the Spooklight's appearance or disappearance can be determined by the observer! He has published a great deal about this and since it is not the intent of this book to explore this topic in detail, I suggest going to Bearden's interesting and informative website. He is the scientist, not me!

If his theory is correct, this would possibly explain why the CSLs either move away from humans or simply disappear when someone tries to approach them. The human mind is powerful and the brain among other things is an electrical generator and it produces electrical fields that perhaps can interact with the other electrical fields that produce Spooklights (if this theory is correct).

Bearden suggests that a cooling of the local environmental temperature may trigger the appearance of a Spooklight because a lower temperature "reduces the photon emission and absorption activity of the environment."

He seems to suggest that more Spooklights will be seen either when there is a decrease in local temperature or during the cooler times of the year.

While I have not bought into all his theories about Spooklights, I have noticed that during the hotter parts of the year, there are fewer SL sightings, even though some of the "better" sightings have occurred in the middle and latter part of summer.

Other interesting aspects of Bearden's theories could explain some anomalies with the Spooklights such as why so few people see them. The best way I can explain it (and I'm guessing that my explanation is a gross oversimplification) is that due to how the various magnetic fields interact with each other, they normally produce an amount of visible light and by nature the phenomena are spherical in shape. And when the light or photons are produced, they are emitted "directionally," which means they travel one way (the idea is that when the photons are produced, they enter virtual state at a "right angle" and therefore are not visible in the sense that a flame would be for example) from their source and if the observer is not at the correct observational vantage point, the Spooklight cannot be seen by the human eye because no photons are being emitted towards the observer. The observer facing the "back side" of the Spooklight would not see it at all because it would not be producing any visible radiation on that "side."

Does this view sound strange? Yes! I also find it very interesting. I'm not sure if this theory has been proven to be valid. However, I did read one internet published article where some researchers were attempting to view and photograph the Marfa Spooklights and had observers on the ground and observers flying over the sighting area in a small airplane. When the ground observers spotted a Spooklight the observers in the airplane flying directly over the Spooklight (the ground observers claimed to have seen the airplane flying directly over the SL), reported they did not see any Spooklights below them or any in the area.

Another interesting thing about Bearden's theories is that if the subterranean currents must flow perpendicular to the train tracks in order to produce the magnetic fields, this would possibly explain why there are only certain sections of tracks were Spooklights can be seen.

It may also be possible that we are perhaps mixing two different phenomena. What if the small lantern size luminous phenomena seen floating above train tracks are not the same kind of luminous phenomena that I am calling Spooklights?

For me, I am not fully convinced there is a direct link with Spooklights and railroad tracks. And yet I cannot ignore the fact that excellent sightings have occurred at them. Perhaps Spooklights are actually attracted to train tracks and actually produced by their magnetic fields. Or maybe these magnetic fields produced by the tracks act as a "trigger" and play a critical role in producing SLs. It just seems to me that there are too many SL sightings in areas where there are not train tracks. I suppose there is much more to learn about this. And who knows, perhaps Bearden's theory about train tracks will prove to be right.

Time exposure of large Spooklight moving across the late evening sky at SLSA2.
Photographed by Wyatt Cox in December 1979.

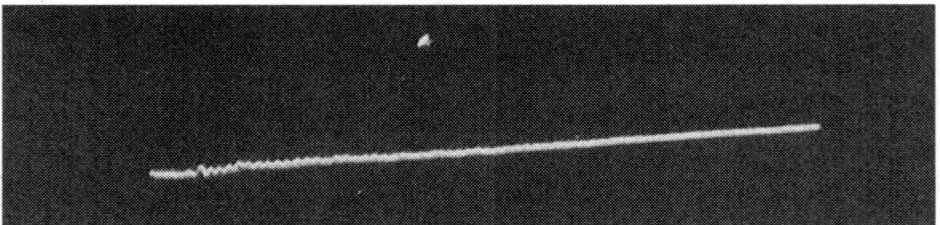

A blow up of a time exposure photo showing the Spooklight move from left to
right. Because the camera's shutter was open for several seconds, I was able to
see how at times the Spooklight would slightly oscillate and at other times would
not. Perhaps the luminous orb needs to reach a certain degree of stability before it
becomes visible. It may also be possible that the Spooklight is still receiving
energy from subterranean piezoelectric discharges.

Explanations

(If I could explain the Spooklights – it would not be a mystery!)

It is awkward for me to write this chapter. Perhaps it is because I am more comfortable telling about sightings and offering data and other people's views than explaining what I personally believe is producing the Spooklight phenomena.

It is not my nature to be uncomfortable with explaining things. In fact I love to teach and explain things. It is just that this SL phenomenon continues to baffle me after all these years. But how can I attempt to write a book of this genre and not have an "Explanations" chapter? So, if I must, then here I go.

In a way I did make a feeble attempt to explain them earlier when I mentioned Tom Bearden's theory about underground electrical currents and railroad tracks. And since I am not a scientist, I realize my limitations. But none the less, I feel the need to elaborate.

I suggest that of all the known Spooklight sighting areas in the U.S., this one is possibly far more active (visibly active) than the others. They can be seen on an almost routine basis and they are larger than most other reported Spooklights. They are not some small and distant light that may appear and flicker for a few brief moments. This phenomenon is repeatable and generally predictable. For a number of reasons, it seems to me that this SL phenomenon is unique in the U.S.

After more than 180 sightings of these SLs, I in all honesty remain mystified as to what they are and how they are produced. While it is easier for me to say what the SLs are not; that does not in and of itself lead me to an understanding of this phenomenon.

However, I have in my mind eliminated various theories suggested due to a lack of direct evidence for their support. For example, I am fully convinced that they are not being produced by technological means, which means the U.S. government is not responsible for their existence seems that for some people, the U.S. Government is responsible for everything that cannot be explained by the general public! Nor are extraterrestrial visitors involved in the SL phenomenon. And the SLs are not associated with occult phenomena. It is my view that the SLs are a unique and natural phenomenon. But this theory still is much too vague to be of value.

And this term "natural" means many things. For instance, are they alive? I examined this provocative thought in the Frequently Asked Questions chapter. While there does appear to be some circumlocutory evidence, I am hesitant to accept this evidence as proof. These SLs do appear to avoid people and buildings, which is baffling (and I have not heard of any explanation that satisfies me with this dilemma) if they are phenomena occurring from the interaction of complex magnetic and electromagnetic fields.

So the question that is begging to be answered is "what are they?" I wish to explore the theory I tend to favor (for now!)

I'll begin by saying that we live on a giant magnet. This magnet which is located at the Earth' core is believed to consist of a rotating mass of iron. Massive amounts of electrical currents constantly flow in this electromagnet and powerful magnetic fields from this magnet extend many miles from its source. It is these potent magnetic fields that help protect us from the deadly radiation emanating from various sources in outer space.

These high reaching and powerful magnetic fields (and our atmosphere) prevents most of the electromagnetic radiation (EM) from space from reaching the Earth. In fact we are constantly bombarded with EM radiation from outer space. And what is electromagnetic radiation? To say it simple: it is energy transmitted through space or through a medium (such as water, air, etc.) in the form of electromagnetic waves. When ever an electric charge vacillates or is accelerated, a disturbance characterized by the existence of electric and magnetic fields propagates from it. This disturbance is referred to as an electromagnetic wave. By its nature, this wave has both electric and magnetic qualities.

This EM radiation has both energy and momentum and needs no medium (such as sound waves) which means it can travel in a vacuum. EM radiation is classified into types according to the frequency of the wave: these waves include radio waves, microwaves, infrared, visible light, ultraviolet, x-rays, and gamma rays.

Only a very small portion of all EM is visible to humans and only a very small range of EM frequencies are visible. But the fact is we are constantly flooded with electromagnetic radiation which originates from multiple sources in outer space.

Now, getting back to earth; we have both EM radiation from outer space and the Earth's powerful magnetic fields. There are other sources of potent electrical energies as well.

One source of electrical energy the Earth manufactures is produced when seismically active areas (and the entire planet is seismically active) release their stress or strain and large quantities of electrical energy (current flow) is discharged from minerals possessing piezoelectric qualities (such as quartz). This geologic stress (called Tectonic Strain) can be caused by various natural activities such as earthquakes, volcanoes, tidal forces, etc. Geologic stress can also be caused by manmade activity such as large dams (there is a very large dam and lake near the sighting areas) and reservoirs. The Earth has many geological faults and is always geologically active. Sometimes the Earth is described not as a big rock but as big ball of Jell-O!

This current flows in a "circuit" of least resistance which may include underground streams. These currents can produce significant electrical and magnetic fields and if there is iron ore (how about railroad tracks!?) involved there could be very powerful magnetic fields. These magnetic fields extend into the atmosphere a considerable distance.

While there has been much written about this Strain Theory, I would suggest for those interested in pursuing this topic to go to:

www.lauretian.ca/neurosci/_research/tectonic_theory.htm

To complicate matters (it does for me!), there are other energies that may be involved. One of these natural occurring energies is called Telluric Currents.

These currents have been observed in both the earth's crust and mantle and are induced by changes in the outer part of the Earth's magnetic field, which are usually caused by the interaction between the solar wind and the ionosphere. Theses underground currents are present all the time and move equator-ward during the daytime and pole-ward during the nighttime.

These telluric currents are very low frequency ranging from .001 to 5 hertz (household current is 60 hertz) and the voltage can range from .2 to more than 500 volts per meter (household voltage is either 115 or 230 volts). This amount of voltage can "push" a lot of current and current can create powerful magnetic field lines.

Can these subterranean currents be causing the Spooklight phenomenon? Can this electromagnetic energy be powerful enough and "focused" to produce some kind of luminous phenomena? Or do these subterranean electrical discharges interact with other natural energies and one of the results is luminous phenomena? And if so how?

After many years of attempting to solve the Cloverdale Spooklight mystery can I state for certain that the piezoelectric theory is responsible for this phenomenon? I really don't know for sure. I do know that the Cloverdale Spooklights are not a result of earthquakes. I am also aware that there is a stable geological fault in northwestern Alabama and this geological fault can and does routinely create tectonic stress. This stress can and does produce subterranean electrical energy.

It sure would be nice for me to be totally confident and offer a simple and easily understandable theory that is neatly packaged and say, this without doubt explains the Spooklight phenomenon. But to honest, I feel uncomfortable in making such a claim. Perhaps these powerful electromagnetic discharges and complex interactions of magnetic fields can "kindle" or charge the air and produce these Cloverdale SLs if the other (which are not known to me) special conditions are present. Perhaps with all these interactions of magnetic fields, a magnetic "string" is created that normally exists horizontally in relation to the earth's surface and these magnetic fields produces a pulsating magnetic bubble on a point on these "strings" and become a visible ball of light.

Perhaps these magnetic "strings" extends both horizontally and directly above a geological fault that either causes the string or produces a magnetic "bubble" that is attached magnetically to the string and it is propelled by either the string's polarity or difference in its electrical charge. Maybe the tectonic strain is the "trigger" to these luminous phenomena. And of course, the magnetic bubble is the Spooklight.

If this view is basically correct, perhaps this could explain why the glowing orbs suddenly appear and disappear. The magnetic bubble

(Spooklight) would suddenly be formed.   Or the energy feeding the Spooklight is not without variation. I am still not sure if a newly formed SL contains all the energy it will have until it disappears or if it is being "fed" by the energy caused by tectonic strain. This could also explain why a SL stops and hovers. There is either a "recharging" of the SL or there is a magnetic field which temporarily holds the SL in place until it is able to break free and then is able to continue moving on the string.

As for the SL that crashed that I mentioned in a different chapter, perhaps the magnetic string lost its integrity and the orb be came separated from it and merely fell to the ground.

Of course, I could be totally wrong about this. While I like this theory I also realize that some of my sightings will be difficult for to explain using the magnetic string theory. The basic claim I am making is that I'm only claiming to be the one who observers the phenomena, not the scientist who explains the phenomenon.

It would seem to me that such a theory could be verified with the necessary technology and other necessary resources. If a team of people were strategically placed in all four sighting areas with cameras and sensitive instruments to detect magnetic fields, then scientific data could be gathered and accurate conclusions drawn.

There does not seem to be a specific spot where the Spooklights first appear.   Sometimes they just suddenly appear in plain view and other times they appear in the distance as though they have been traveling for a while. But they do appear in their "path."

And part of the puzzle for me is if the energies and conditions exist to produce a SL, then why is only one visible orb produced at a time. Why not two or three or even more? But no, just one and only on rare occasions are two seen in the sky at the same time. And even then, except for one case I know of, they are not in the same flight path. They are in different parts of the sky and at different altitudes. Only once, did I observe two SLs at the same altitude and traveling in opposite directions on a "collision" course. And if there is enough energy to produce two eight-foot diameter balls of light, then why not more? Like I said earlier, everybody loves a mystery!

Other questions abound. Why are they always the same size? They are normally with rare exception about eight-feet in diameter. Even the Marfa, Texas Spooklights vary greatly in size. And the other Spooklights elsewhere are usually reported to be quite small, from 1-2 feet in diameter. But not the Cloverdale Spooklights. There is little variance with the yellowish-orange orbs.

I'm not completely sure how to incorporate the Tectonic Strain theory with the Cloverdale Spooklight Phenomenon. But of all the theories I have explored, this one is the most difficult to rule out.

For an excellent discussion of a fascinating theory which might explain what produces the Marfa Spooklights, I highly recommend the book, Night Orbs, by James Bunnell. It is published by Lacey Publishing Company and is for me a "must read" for anyone interested in the mysterious luminous phenomena reported by hundreds of credible witnesses near Marfa, Texas during the past several decades.

Above is a time exposure of Spooklight seen at SLSA2 and was moving towards Cloverdale.

Below are two photos of the back border of the Old Prison Camp. Several Spooklights have been seen within a mile of this area. Train tracks are less than 100 yards from the camp.

My Three Best SL Sightings

The Spooklight and the Train (and tracks!)

One of my most extraordinary sightings of a Spooklight occurred in late August of Greg and I were in a large field about six miles east of Cloverdale. There was a set of frequently used railroad tracks at the edge of the field. On the other side of the railroad tracks was what Greg and I called the "old abandoned prison camp" which consisted of some old dilapidated buildings and several acres surrounded by a security fence. Years ago, this place was a minimum security prison and from what I have heard, it ceased to be used sometime back in the early 1960s. A casual observer could easily think it was abandoned because no one was stationed at the prison and no maintenance was being performed on the buildings. By the mid 1970s, many of the buildings had either collapsed or were on the verge of doing so.

Anyway, about one hundred feet past the north side of the prison camp was the railroad tracks. Greg and I were not in the old prison camp but were in a field nearby where we could be at the highest point in the sighting area. We had been in this field many times and experience had shown us this was an excellent location. Of the approximately 180 Spooklights Greg and I have seen, I would estimate that more than 140 have been seen at this one location.

One of the unusual characteristics of the SLs seen at this location was that their appearance was sometimes predictable. We knew from experience that after 10:00 p.m. the likelihood of spotting a SL was not favorable. So at 10:00 p.m. Greg and I decided to call it a night and I dismantled our camera from the tripod and walked back to my car which was about 300 feet away.

When I finished loading the equipment, I walked back to see if Greg was ready to leave. Normally, I would go to his house first and then we would proceed to the viewing area. Since driving two cars was not needed, we usually rode together.

Just as I returned to where Greg was standing, I heard a train in the far distance. We could tell the train was coming from the east by its noise. Within a few moments we noticed the bright head light pierce through the darkness and it was heading our way. Greg and I joked that we would stay and watch the train pass by so that way we could honestly say we saw "something" that night! As soon as the train came into sight, for what ever reason, I turned and look to my right and I instantly yelled at Greg,

"There's a light!" We were at first speechless as we stared at the glowing orb.

About ½ miles away from Greg and I was a very bright Spooklight just hanging in the air – directly above the railroad tracks. The orb was about eight feet in diameter and very its typical yellowish-orange color. The SL appeared to be suspended about 30 feet above the railroad tracks. It was completely motionless. It was truly a wondrous thing to see!

To say the least, Greg and I were dumbfounded. We had never seen a SL hover directly over the rail road tracks. We had seen a similar Spooklight floating near the ground within a half mile away about a year before. We were just like a deer hunter who comes face to face with the perfect 10 point deer – the kind of deer only one could dream about. Some times a deer hunter is completely mesmerized by the deer and never thinks about shooting it. And from what I've been told, these types of deer sightings happen fairly frequently.

Greg and I were both like the deer hunter. We just watched for a few seconds not saying anything. Then we began to look to our left and see the train approaching and then look back to the SL. It just hung in the air; the orb did not move, or change its brightness. Was it being forced to remain directly above the tracks by naturally occurring magnetic or did it "choose" to be there and to patiently wait for the train? These were questions that we later asked each other (often).

What seemed like hours were actually just a few moments; the train was directly in front of us moving rapidly down the tracks to our right. We guessed the train was moving at its normal speed – which we estimated to be about 25-35 MPH. If the train engineer saw the SL, he made no effort to slow down or sound his deafening horn. I still don't believe the engineer was aware of the Spooklight's presence.

And then the unimaginable happened. At the very moment the train engine passed directly under the SL, the orange ball of plasma instantly began moving down the tracks at exactly the same speed of the train! It was like they were inseparably and invisibly connected or possible magnetically linked to each other. The train and the Spooklight keep moving farther away from Greg and me until after about a minute or slightly longer, they were both out of sight. The SL did not disappear rather it just followed the train until it was outside of our view. For the entire time the Spooklight followed the train it stayed in sync with its engine, never changing its relative position of about 30 feet above the tracks.

To me, this was the "this is something I will never forget" experience. Why did I not run back to the car and get the camera? I kick myself every time I think of this sighting. Of course, Greg and I had no idea what the Spooklight was going to do or if the train would respond to its presence. This is the only time we ever saw a train and a Spooklight at the same time. We have never seen a SL hover over train tracks or be associated with a train except in this case. (We were told by a UFO researcher that Spooklights were sometimes seen above the railroad tracks in the small town of Elora, Tennessee, which is just a short distance north of Huntsville).

Why did the SL materialize right above the train tracks with a train approaching? And why did the SL react as it did when the train was directly below it? Either the orb reacted to the electrical field produced by the train's generators or by the orbs' magnetic field reacting to the tons of steel of the train.

Why did the Spooklight maintain its elevation in relation to the ground after the train passed under it? For what ever reasons, the SL hovered about 30 feet from the ground prior to the train's arrival. And it remained at the same elevation when the train was under it. What energies were present to cause the SL to follow the train but did not cause it to change it relative distance from the locomotive?

And also, why did the Spooklight "appear" on the tracks when it did. For that matter, why did it appear directly above the center of the tracks at all? And what are the odds that it would materialize just a few moments before a train would appear? Why not materialize a few moments after the train had passed? Another somewhat perplexing question for Greg and me which was of a philosophical nature was: why did the SL materialize in such a location and at the right time for us to witness it (without a camera)? Did the SL "know" the train was coming? The problem with answering one of these questions is that it generates many more questions! It just doesn't' generate a lot of answers!

As mentioned earlier, according to Thomas Bearden, (well known theoretical physicist) he believes that it may be possible for the earth's electrical fields to react to train tracks and by this interaction produce an energy (he calls it a hyper field) fields above train tracks and luminous phenomena can then be produced inside this hyper field.

Other puzzling aspects of this sighting continue to baffle me. Was the orb absorbing energy from the train's electrical system? Did the Spooklight actually "appear" moments prior to the train's arrival or had it been there for a longer period of time; just not visible? If so, what caused the orb to go from being invisible to visible?

I remain unsure of the science behind this phenomenon. But I sure wish I had my camera out that night!

The Meeting Of The Two

On the night of 28 September of 1979 I had another one of my three most remarkable Spooklight sightings and I am still as mystified today as I was then. I was at the edge of a large field that bordered Highway 17, less than a mile from the Alabama/Tennessee State line. Several SLs had been seen at this area and I was there alone that night.

It was almost dark and I did not have any camera equipment set up at the time. The sun was setting but it was not quiet dark yet. It was about 5:45 p.m. and the sky was clear. There to my far left (west) I noticed a bright Spooklight and it was moving eastward very slowly. It was fairly high – much higher than the tree tops and maybe more than ½ mile away. It appeared to be a "normal" SL because of its color and apparent size. After about 30 seconds or so I looked to my far right (west) and to my total amazement there was another SL! This Spooklight was not only a "normal" one but it was also moving slowly towards the west and it was at the same altitude as the one to my right! It was evident they were either on an intersect or collision course! This is not something Greg or I had ever seen before. We have on rare occasions seen more than one SL in the sky at one time, but never on the same flight path.

As I watched, totally mesmerized by the two large and bright SLs, I was sure they were going to collide. What really happened, I not exactly sure. As they approached each other, neither one changed their color, speed or altitude. At the moment I thought they would collide, something happened. They both suddenly stopped moving. But only one Spooklight could be seen! Either they merged together and became one or one SL stopped directly behind the other. But either way, I had never seen this happen before.

The glowing orb I could see just hung motionless in the sky. No change in color or size. It just hung there. What seemed like a long time but was really about 20-25 seconds, the other SL "emerged." Either the other Spooklight really did emerge or it simply came out from behind the SL me. I suspect the latter happened. But what I don't know is if the SL that came out from the west reversed its course and traveled west or if the one that came of the east simply continued on it east to west journey.

When the other Spooklight reappeared, they both began moving slowly-at the same speed as before. They continued on their flight until they both were out of sight. Except for what I just described, they were in every sense of the word "normal" SLs. This sighting lasted for about five minutes. If I only had my camera!

Now I wonder that since these two Spooklight were "normal," do others "merge" as well? If so, then why?

The Spooklight that "crashed"

In October of 1977, we witnessed a bright orange Spooklight "crash" into a large wooded area near the "old prison camp." Actually, there four witnesses. Greg and I had invited two friends out to a very large field where several Spooklights had been seen by us and on different occasions by the property owner.

On this night, we were fortunate that the weather was cooperative; there were no clouds and the fall air was pleasant. While the stars were shining bright, the moon had not yet risen.

At about 9:00 p.m. we spotted a Spooklight traveling eastward just above some trees in the distance. The SL was moving at its normal speed but was decreasing its altitude. Normally, the altitude is either maintained or increased. The SL was bright orange and completely silent. It was also large – about 8 feet in diameter or possibly more. As it moved eastward, the bright orb was also getting closer to us. We realized that something was amiss with this orb because it was changing altitude very quickly.

We were not sure if it was going to crash or "land." Since Greg and I at this time entertained the idea that they may be intelligently controlled, we really did not know what to expect.

But down it came. When the SL was just below tree top level and we were maybe ½ mile away, it entered into a heavily wooded area and at that point we lost sight of it. At the time we four all thought it went behind a small hill or went into a ravine. But we all witnessed it go to ground level before disappearing.

After a brief and excited discussion as to what to do, we all ran through the field to the wooded area to find the Spooklight. Since we did not know what it was or if there were hazards associated with it, we proceeded with much caution when we came to the edge of the woods. Talk about an adrenalin rush!

We entered the wooded area looking for a bright orange light, but saw only darkness and trees There was no Spooklight to be found. What happened to the bright orange orb? That question was repeated several times. We were completely perplexed. The only possible explanation is that the Spooklight's energy had significantly diminished and was below the minimum level to sustain its existence.

We were all so excited! We actually had seen a Spooklight "crash!" Yet, it wasn't exactly a crash. There was no object on the ground. We did not hear the SL impact the ground. Neither the ground nor vegetation was disturbed. In fact, two days later (during the daytime) when Greg and I went back to the "crash" sight, we diligently searched the area with the hopes of finding something unusual. We left the wooded area perplexed because we found no evidence of any kind to suggest anything unusual had occurred. The Spooklight apparently produced no significant heat (at least no significant heat at the time of impact) nor was it a physical object which would have affected what ever it came in contact with. Or possibly the SL became unstable and its energy dissipated just before it "crashed."

This sighting caused me to ask more questions. For instance: Was the SL actually on the ground but not visible? If so, as much time we spent at the "crash site" we would have walked through the invisible orb. If we did, we were unaware of that happening. How does a SL lose its energy so quickly? Perhaps its energy source is underground and is not constant. So many questions.

A one minute time exposure (above) of a large Spooklight near SLSA3. The camera was mounted on a tripod and a shutter release cable was used to minimize camera movement. Spooklights may appear to travel in a straight line but actually moves somewhat erratically as this photo demonstrates.

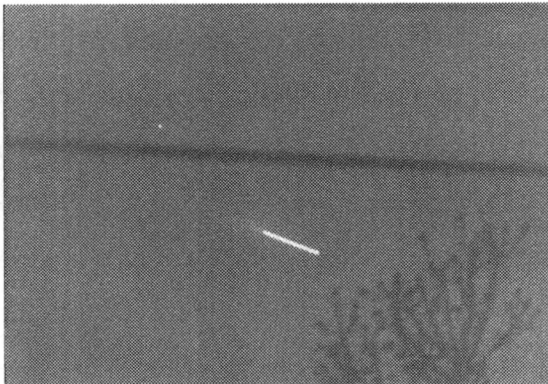

Time exposure on left shows a bright yellowish-orange Spooklight at GLSA2 moving to the right (west) and it appears to be leaving some kind of luminous discharge.

Is There A Spooklight "Corridor?"

(or how not to determine the size of a Spooklight Corridor)

Based on our research we have a general idea to the location and size of this "corridor" as we call it (some call it "window"). Or so we would like to think.

Perhaps there is no corridor but only "windows." Assuming there is a corridor, it appears to be a fairly long (about 20 miles) rectangle with perhaps several "windows" or maybe more accurately there are "paths" where the majority of the CSLs are seen. As far as the SLs are concerned, Greg and I are not really sure of its boundaries, but we do suspect that the boundaries are "fixed" and we base this on the long history of Spooklights being seen year after year in the same location – even in the same fields for more than three decades.

While Greg and I spent more of our time and energy in watching and attempting to learn what we observed, we spent less time trying to figure out where all the places may be where they can be seen. But we did try to determine how big of a "window" existed and how far a Spooklight could travel while in its visible form. We know from personal experience SLs can be seen as far north as the Alabama/Tennessee State line and almost as far south as Florence, at least in the areas we conducted most of our field investigations.

Based on numerous UFO reports and interviews, we believe the Cloverdale Spooklight Corridor extends at least as far east as Lexington which is just south of the Tennessee State line and as far west as Cloverdale. It extends as for north as Tennessee and as far south to Cloverdale. This would mean the corridor would be more than 20 miles long and maybe five miles wide; of course, we have no hard proof to validate our claims. Inside this corridor seems to be several small "windows" where the majority of the SLs are seen. There most likely are many other pockets that Greg and I are unaware of. It is also possible that there are not small windows but the SLs may actually travel a very long distance, part of the time visible and part of the time invisible (not producing visible light).

For a while, the idea of a corridor intrigued us and we were hoping we could verify its existence and obtain a better estimate of its size. Greg and I on one occasion did try to discover if this idea was true. Back in 1980, Greg and I drove to Elora, Tennessee to take a chance on watching a large red Spooklight that we learned about from a woman in Huntsville. She seemed familiar with the Elora Spooklight phenomena and knew we were interested in going there to investigate the site. She claimed several people have reported a large triangle or diamond shaped red light floating above some railroad tracks near Elora.

We knew the specific location of the alleged sightings and what really piqued our interest was that the SL was large and that it had been seen to float above some railroad tracks. We really wanted to know if SLs were being seen in other areas and if this phenomenon were related. We also wanted to know if there is a direct association with Spooklights and train tracks.

We arrived at the location about 9:00 p.m. and when knew from what we had been told that the best time to spot this red orb was around 10:00 p.m. or later. I actually parked my car just a few feet away from the tracks and got out to assess the area. We were at the railroad crossing where the Spooklights had been observed. Of course it was pitch dark; no moon or nearby lights. The entire area was heavily wooded and we were right dab in the middle of nowhere! This was actually good because it allowed us to spot lights easier but it was bad because we were in an unknown location at night and could not see anything!

We had been there for a while and had not seen any thing interesting. Then we heard something. We were not sure what it was, but there in the woods, we heard a light shuffling noise in the distance. It wasn't loud but we both could hear it. We could not accurately estimate how far away we were from what was causing the odd sound. Then we realized that someone or something was walking in the woods! What we heard was definitely the sounds caused by feet walking in heavy woods. Could it have been a deer? I have heard deer walk on leaves and to me what I was hearing was not the sound of a walking deer!

One thing was sure- the odd an unnerving sound was getting closer. Greg and I began to talk much louder to each other so that what ever was making the noise would have to hear us talking. We figured if it was a deer it would scare it away. We even used our flashlights to attempt to pierce the surrounding darkness but did not see what was causing the unsettling noise. But what ever was making the sound was still getting much closer. We were fully aware that in the blackness of the night, what ever it was would have to be almost within a few feet before we could spot it moving.

We became very concerned (scared!) and we yelled out to our unknown and uninvited guest that we had stopped at the train tracks to watch the train go by (which was partially true). If it was a person he would know why we were there. And where we parked was on the road's right of way so we were not trespassing on private property.

There was no response to our shouts. But that walking in the woods sound was getting much closer, for we had parked at the very edge of the woods. It was obvious to us that what ever was making those walking sounds were just a few yards away. And since the front of my car was pointing in the opposite direction of the woods, it would have served no purpose to turn the head lights on. We were both aware that Bigfoot had been reported by several witnesses about seven miles away near the town of Flintville. As the noise became closer, we both were quickly thinking about the possibility of there was either a person or a Bigfoot approaching us. I'm guessing that at this time rational thinking was yielding to vivid and undisciplined imaginations.

We were not sure what to do. To be honest, we panicked at the same time and we both quickly jumped into my car and locked the doors. We hurriedly decided now was the time to make a hasty exit. And exit we did! We drove a few miles south to Huntsville and spent the night in a motel room.

We did learn that from about 1976 to 2002, dozens (not just a few) of witnesses had reported either spotting Bigfoot or finding some kind of physical evidence of Bigfoot. And to add to the story, several of the Bigfoot was reported to have acted aggressively towards the witnesses and to some farm animals. An excellent article about the Bigfoot sightings in Flintville (a small town about five miles northwest of Elora) can be seen at: www.bigfootencounters.com/articles/tennessee.htm.

Could there have been a Bigfoot checking Greg and me out? Was someone engaged in some nighttime hunting merely stomping around in the woods? Or was it a deer? We really don't know. And then we wondered are Spooklights and Bigfoot somehow connected? Is there a paranormal component to all of this? Or do Greg and I ask too many questions? Like I said in the beginning of the book – everybody loves a mystery!

But anyway, Greg and I are not sure how large this Corridor is. Perhaps it is much longer and wider that what we have estimated. Or maybe there is no corridor, but only a few small "windows" or "pockets" that are not directly connected. One thing was for sure, our motivation for determining the length of the Spooklight Corridor quickly decreased as the distance of those footsteps from us we heard also decreased!

Our courage returned to us the next day (is that a surprise?) and we went back to the train tracks in Elora during the day time and looked around where we had been the previous night. We did not find any evidence of Bigfoot. Nor did we find any deer tracks.

Time exposure photo (left) of a Spooklight seen at GLSA1 just as the sun was setting. This one was high in the sky and the moon is clearly visible.

Time exposure of Spooklight (right) observed at GLSA1 shortly after dark. Trees in the foreground can barely be seen. It was bright and moved slowly to the west and was
in sight for about five minutes.

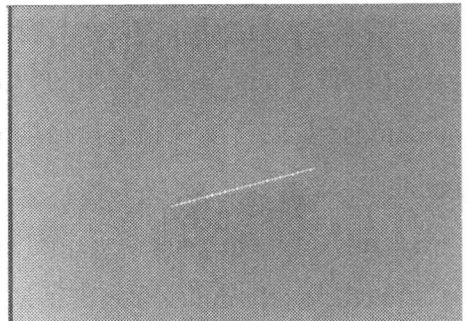

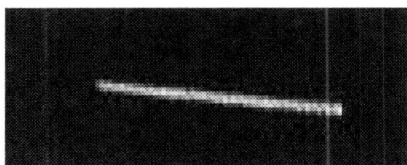

A blow up of a time exposure of a Spooklight oscillating as it crosses the sky at GLSA3. The camera was mounted on a tripod and a shutter release cable was used.

What about the Taos Hum (aka Earth Hum)?

The "Taos Hum" or Earth Hum is a very strange phenomenon. This mysterious low pitched sound is called the Taos Hum because it was first reported to be heard in the small town of Taos, New Mexico. It appears that very low frequency sounds are generated by unknown natural means in certain (but not many) locations throughout the world, including some in the United States. It is usually heard in quiet locations and the persons reporting the Taos Hum usually describes the sound as that of a diesel engine running in the distance. Generally those that report hearing this nocturnal auditory disturbance are in agreement with what it sounds like, but the perceived intensity depends upon the person.

The Taos Hum involves an invasive low frequency sounds (possibly in the 40-100 hertz range) and is thus far undetectable by most conventional microphones.

There are several odd things about the Taos Hum. First, it is not a constant sound; when it will be produced is part of the mystery. When it is heard, it is normally during and after sunset. Second, not everyone is able to hear it. One Hum researcher suggests that only about 2-3% of the population can hear it.

Some people perceive the hum constantly while others hear it intermittently. Some barely detect it while others find it a serious distraction and even interferes with their sleep and concentration. Several theories have been suggested and they include:

Man-made noise that has become distorted and amplified, especially the very low frequency noise. This theory for numerous reasons had not gained significant support.   Some suggest it is possible that infrasound produced by geological activity may be producing the phenomenon. Complex energy fields from various electromagnetic sources (natural and man made) are somehow interacting and producing this low frequency hum.

Others suggest that solar wind is interacting with the earth's atmosphere and producing low frequency vibrations. Or possibly low frequency communication systems employed by the US government is somehow producing the Taos Hum. Perhaps our Government is artificially heating the ionosphere by huge ionoshperic heating systems (for more info – do a web search for HAARP).   There is supposedly one of these facilities located in northern Alaska and according to some conspiracy minded folks its purpose is to significantly alter the earth's weather systems.

But why do I even mention the Taos Hum in this book? Is it related to the Cloverdale Spooklights and if so, how? Before I heard of the term Taos Hum, I would occasion hear what I thought was a diesel engine running in the distance while at the CGSA4. I thought that it was rather odd that a diesel engine would be running for a long time at night and be heard from such a far distance. After a while I thought that maybe it was not that strange. The sound was not loud enough to be a distraction or nuisance, just loud enough that I clearly hear it.

One night while Greg and I were watching the sky for Spooklights, I began to hear the hum and after a few minutes of listening to the odd distant noise, I asked Greg what could be causing the constant "diesel engine noise" that I (and I assumed he did too) was hearing. And based on his vague and hesitant answer, it was clear that he did not hear the strange noise. And that got me to thinking.

I make no attempt to explain the Taos Hum but only wish to offer my musings. It seems to me that the Hum is not man-made but is some kind of natural phenomenon.   Whether the energy that produces the Hum is generated is subterranean or atmospheric in nature (or a combination of both), there definitely seems to be an electromagnetic component involved. And if electromagnetism is involved, then is the Hum somehow related to Spooklights? Hopefully more research will determine if this theory is valid.

In the meantime, the Taos Hum is just one more (or is it?) aspect of the Cloverdale Spooklight phenomenon.

Selected Websites

(I am not necessarily endorsing these websites but include them as a resource for those who may wish to gain additional information and perspectives)

Taos Hum

www.eskimo.com

www.earthpulse.com

UFO

www.Auforc.com

www.MUFON.com

Spooklights

www.ghost.org/ghostlights/ghostlights.html

www.earthlights.org

www.paranoraml.about.com

www.wyattknows.com

www.lemurteam.com

www.prairieghosts.com

www.hessdalen.org

Sites I frequently browse

www.cheniere.org

www.forteantimes.com

www.mysterious-america.net

Time exposure photo of a bright Spooklight seen at SLSA2. It was large and moved slowly towards the west. Photograph by Wyatt Cox

Glossary

Earth Hum

See section called "What about the Taos Hum"

Spooklight

A large spherical shaped ball of light that suddenly appears and disappears. They usually glow brightly in the night and many emit a pulsating yellowish-orange light. What they are remains a mystery. They are sometimes called Ghostlights, Aerial Luminous Phenomena, Geophysical Luminous Phenomena, etc.

HUM

See Earth Hum

Piezoelectric

According to Wikipedia, "Piezoelectricity is the ability of crystals to generate a voltage in response to applied mechanical stress." The basic thought in regards to the Spooklights is that substantial deposits of quartz and similar mineral are located beneath the surface and experience various amounts of stress due to natural forces which may include an active geological fault, tidal forces, etc.

When the mechanical stress varies on these crystals, electrical current is produced. These electrical fields in the presence of water, iron, etc. can create strong electromagnetic fields which are somehow responsible for the formation and movement of the Spooklights.

Orange Spooklights

They are about eight-foot diameter glowing orbs that comprise the majority of all Spooklights seen in the Cloverdale/Lexington Corridor. They are usually a bright yellowish-orange or orange sphere and can be seen high in the sky or hovering a couple of feet from the ground. They are unaffected by the wind, are silent and pulsates.

White Spooklights

Rarely seen in the Cloverdale/Lexington Corridor and are smaller than the Orange SLs.

Blue Spooklights

Rarely reported in the Cloverdale/Lexington Corridor and are smaller than the Orange SLs.

Marfa, Texas

One of the most well known areas in the United States to view Spooklights. Many articles have been published as well as made for TV documentaries. James Bunnell has published a book called Night Orbs which documents and attempts to explain the Marfa Spooklight phenomenon.

Plasmoid Phenomena

A coherent structure of plasma and magnetic fields that may be responsible for the SLs. Plasma is basically a gas that is heated to the point where it begins to release electrons and a magnetic field is the region around an electric current, electric field or magnet in which magnetic forces exist.

Brown Mountain, North Carolina

Brown Mountain is perhaps one of the best known areas to view Spooklights. Many made for TV documentaries have been produced about the Brown Mountain phenomenon.

Spooklight Window

There seems to be various "windows" or spots where Spooklights can be found in various places on earth. The reasons for these "windows" are unclear (at least to me!), yet the evidence seems to suggest they are real. In these "windows" is where SLs will be seen.

Notes

1. If you travel to Cloverdale to view the SLs – please beware of the following:

A. The northern part of Alabama receives about 50 inches of rain a year and thunderstorms are not uncommon.

B. Poisonous snakes (Rattle Snakes and Copperheads) make the woods and fields their home – thankfully snake bits are very uncommon – but be aware!

C. Black Widow spiders also live in northern Alabama.

D. And as most parts of the south – there are Fire Ants. Don't step on one of their mounds!

E. Winters can be cold and wet!

F. Please be respectful and do not trespass on private property.

2. Is There A Spooklight Corridor Extending From Marfa, Texas To Brown Mountain, North Carolina?

In reviewing many articles, websites, etc, I find that some Spooklight researchers tend to report that active Spooklight sighting areas are a relatively small area and is an independent phenomenon which is unrelated to other similar Spooklight sighting areas. Some researches seek to find some kind of geological or even paranormal anomaly unique to that area that may be producing the Spooklight.

For many years I also subscribed to this view and only read about other sighting areas to hopefully learn more about the Cloverdale Spooklights. I learned that there are many similarities among the various Spooklight sighting areas.

While there was no apparent link between different Spooklight sighting areas (i.e. Marfa, Texas, and Brown Mountain, North Carolina), I could not shake the feeling that surely there is some commonality that exists between these areas separated by hundreds of miles.

It is easy to see that the similarities are many and the dissimilarities seem few. And a portion of the unique characteristics of some Spooklights could be accounted for by using conventional wisdom; such as a few of the Marfa Spooklights have been proven to be automobile headlights seen in the distance. I must add that I am not a Spooklight debunker. It is my view that most of the Marfa Spooklights are genuine and not manmade or misidentifications.

As my knowledge increased about this phenomenon, my views of their origins also evolved. I began to explore other ideas. One day while looking at an atlas of the United States, I wanted to find precisely where

Marfa, Texas is located. This is one of the better places to see Spooklights in the U.S. Another excellent location is Brown Mountain, North Carolina. But what I noticed actually startled me. If I were to draw a straight line from Marfa to Brown Mountain, that line would go right through Gurdon, Arkansas which has an AGSA, and also through the Cloverdale, Alabama AGSAs! Could this be a coincidence?

It sure seems odd to me that at least four AGSAs can be crossed by simply drawing a straight line! After much study, I am still trying to decide what this means – or if it means anything at all. Perhaps this is a coincidence. Yet I have a tendency to think differently. However, at this time I only have circumstantial evidence (and a hunch or two) but the idea is very fascinating to say the least.

Just for the sake of discussion: What if my suspicions are correct and there exists some kind of long Spooklight corridor or magnetic line for these Spooklights. I am not saying that this corridor would begin at Marfa and ends at Brown Mountain; it would most likely is much longer. Nor do I know how wide this alleged corridor is, but it seems to be it is not much more than 15-20 miles and for various reasons, there seems to be a number of "windows" in this corridor. And I am not suggesting that Spooklights can be seen everywhere inside this corridor; for it seems that for reasons I do not understand there could be several active windows in various locations inside the corridor. There would need to be an additional energy source to act as the trigger to produce the luminous phenomena.
The big question is: if there is a corridor, then what is causing it?

Continuing on with our hypothetical scene: I would suspect there may be some kind of "energy line" which exists underground and which interacts with other natural conditions such as seismic strain, large amounts of underground water acting as an electrical circuit, quartz or similar minerals which are capable of producing high voltages given ideal conditions and possibly iron ore present near the surface (or rail road tracks?). Additional research may prove there are other Spooklights or nocturnal UFOs seen along this "energy line."

This "energy line" could be produced by the earth's solid metal core spinning in an outer, liquid core of molten iron. The idea is that there are high levels of electric current circulating in the earth's core and these currents produce large "directional" electromagnetic fields. These "directional" fields are the "energy lines." Is this theory valid? Someone smarter than me will need to weigh in on this one.

Then again, there is no empirical evidence that I am aware of suggesting there is a direct connection between the Marfa Spooklights and the Cloverdale Spooklights. But it is very odd to say the least that all four SLSA can be connected by merely drawing a straight line on a map!

3. Spooklights and airplanes

There has been some discussion as to where there is any link between the Cloverdale Spooklights and airplanes. There are two thoughts I wish to explore. One is, on nights when Greg and I had some very good

Spooklight sightings we would also see lots of airplanes. We joked about if we are going to spot a SL when in a viewing area just because we saw lots of planes. When I say lots of planes, I mean about 12-20 in a time period of about five hours.

Another odd idea that has surfaced and perhaps evidence supporting it has come from some researchers involved in the Marfa, Texas Spooklights is that the orbs as bright as they are cannot be seen when the observer is above them. This may not make any sense to rational people like myself, but one interesting article I read on the internet regarding the Marfa Lights was that while field investigators were on the ground observing a SL, another investigator was in a small plane flying over the location of the SL and the pilot and investigator were unable not sight the luminous orb. Is it possible that if the Spooklight's energy source originates from under the earth's surface and it focal point is several feet above the ground, then could it be that the visible light somehow is not seen when directly above the SL? Maybe the visible light does not easily penetrate the pulsating magnetic field of the Spooklight. Don't know – just a thought. But this view would be consistent with Bearden's theory on the generation of Spooklights which I mentioned earlier.

However, if there is validity to this theory, then it could explain why there are not more SL sightings in the Cloverdale area. And since they are not solid objects, the radar at the nearby airports would not be able to detect them.

References

Excalibur Briefing – Thomas Bearden, Strawberry Press, 1980, pages 20-21.

Night Orbs – James Bunnell, Lacey Publishing Company, 2003

Sky Creatures: Living UFOs – Trevor James Constable, Pocket Books, 1976, page 13.

Handbook of Unusual Natural Phenomena – William Corliss, The Source Book Project, 1977.

Illuminating the Darkness: The Mystery of Spooklights – Dale Kaczmarek, Ghost Research Society Press, 2003

UFO and Bigfoot Sightings in Alabama – Wyatt Cox, Booklocker, 2004

Specula – Wyatt Cox and Greg Keeton, Vol. 3, Number 3, July-Sept. 1980, pages 9-13.

Specula – Wyatt Cox and Greg Keeton, Vol. 3, Number 2, April-June, 1980, pages 8-18.

Specula – Wyatt Cox and Greg Keeton, Vol. 2, Number 2, April-June 1979, pages 19-22.

Earthlights – Paul Devereux, Turnstone Press, 1982

Index

Spooklights: The Amazing Cloverdale, Alabama Spooklight Mystery is a fascinating and persuasive book that summarizes and documents years of field research into the Spooklights seen near Cloverdale, Alabama. Written by an experienced Spooklight investigator who has witnessed more than 180 Spooklights and argues there may be powerful geophysical produced pockets of energy that are responsible for the formation of these large eight-foot diameter yellowish-orange glowing orbs. Wyatt's extensive research provides new information, new insights and compelling evidence about their possible origins. This book provides information startling photographic evidence which may be unfamiliar to many researchers but and will be of interest to laymen and scientist alike. It provides information for the Cloverdale Spooklight seekers regarding the best locations, when to go, probabilities of observing a large eight-foot diameter orb, Spooklight characteristics, patterns and behavior.

This book is a "must" for those seriously interested in Spooklight phenomena.

Facts about the Cloverdale Spooklights

They are large – about eight-feet in diameter and are very bright

They can be seen on an almost routine basis

Some fly very near to the ground

Some Spooklights are seen near the local railroad tracks

Sometimes as many as five Spooklights are seen in a single night

Many will stop and hover for unknown reasons

Some seem to "know" when people are nearby

About the Author

Wyatt Cox has investigated the Cloverdale Spooklight phenomenon for several years and has personally witnessed more than 180 Spooklight events. He was born in Florence, Alabama and has a B.A. degree in theology. Wyatt is the author of *UFO and Bigfoot Sightings in Alabama.* He is currently living in South Carolina and is employed by the U.S. Army Corps of Engineers.

Wyatt can be contacted at: wyattknows@yahoo.com

Coming Soon From

Ghost Research Society Press

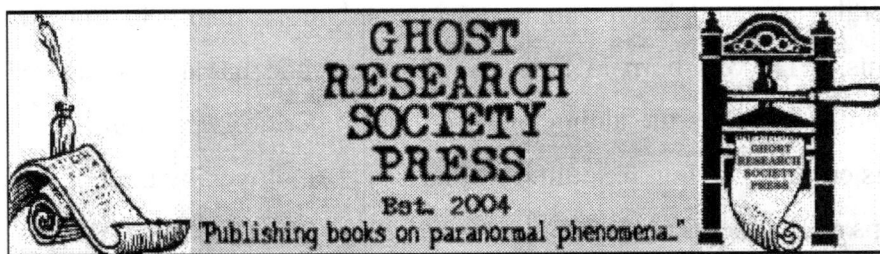

GHOST
RESEARCH
SOCIETY
PRESS
Est. 2004
"Publishing books on paranormal phenomena."

FIELD GUIDE TO MICHIGAN HAUNTINGS
"If you are seeking a haunted peninsula, look around you"
By Jim Graczyk

FIELD GUIDE TO HAUNTED CHURCHES, SYNAGOGUES
and CATHEDRALS
"Ghostly activity on Sacred Ground from across the U. S."
By Dale Kaczmarek

Homepage of the Ghost Research Society Press
http://www.ghostresearch.org/press

Visit Jim Graczyk's webpage at:
http://www.ghostguides.com